Gastronomic
DICTIONARY

Spanish - English

Thomas Harmsworth

Thomas Harmsworth's
Gastronomic Dictionary
Spanish-English
THOMAS HARMSWORTH PUBLISHING COMPANY

© 2004 Thomas Harmsworth Publishing Company
First Published 2004
Reprinted 2006

The publisher regrets that it can accept no responsibility for any errors or
omissions within this publication, or for any expenses or loss thereby caused.

A few words are included in this dictionary which are asserted to be proprietary
names. The presence or absence of such names should not be considered to affect
the legal status of any such names or trade marks.

British Library Cataloguing-in-Publication Data. A catalogue record of this book is
available from the British Library.

In the same series:
French-English
Spanish-English

ISBN 0-948807-56-3
ISSN 1741-3370

Printed in Great Britain by
Creeds the Printers, Broadoak, Bridport DT6 5NL

Introduction

The Spanish-speaking world is extensive. A *Gastronomic Dictionary* Spanish-English must cover not only Spain itself, but other vast regions: Central America, Mexico, The Caribbean (West Indies) and the whole of South America (except Brazil, which is Portuguese-speaking). And South America breaks up linguistically into smaller regions, the largest of which is the Southern Cone (Cono Sur) (Argentina, Paraguay, Uruguay, Chile). Others include the River Plate area, the Andes, and even individual countries. In these parts, it will be noticed that certain words are specific to the region.

Pronounciation
Castilian is regarded as the purest Spanish. It is spoken by those in a large area of central-north Spain, and regardless of background. Each syllable is clearly articulated. It has one basic anomaly - 'c' before 'e' or 'i' is pronounced 'th.' 'Cinco' (five) is pronounced 'thinko.' (It stems from the days when a Spanish king had a lisp, and all his courtiers imitated his pronounciation!). In other parts of the Spanish-speaking world, 'c' is pronounced 's'. 'Z' is also pronounced 'th', except in South America, where it is pronounced 's.'

In South America there is a tendency to drop the final 's' on a word. So 'dos' (two) is pronounced 'dor.' 'C' before 'e' or 'i' is pronounced 's;' and 'll' is pronounced 'y' ('calle' (street) is pronounced 'car-yay'). In some regions of South America 'll' is pronounced 'ge' (like in garage). It may be difficult for the traveller with a smattering of Castilian Spanish to understand South American Spanish, but the South Americans can usually be relied on to understand your Castilian!

Accents: for words ending in a vowel or ~n or ~s, place the stress on the last syllable but one; e.g. aroma (of wine: bouquet). For words ending in a consonant, other than ~n or ~s, place the stress on the last syllable; e.g. alcohol (alcohol). If this rule does not apply, an accent is placed on the stressed syllable; e.g. platón (serving dish).

Most spanish things are masculine; unless they end ~a, ~ión, ~d, ~z.

In spanish ñ is treated as a separate letter of the alphabet, and comes at the end of n. (Strictly, ch and ll are separate letters too, as is rr, but this last would not have a separate dictionary entry).

Diminutives, augmentatives
Many spanish words have diminutive (or augmentative) counterparts. Cuchara (spoon); cucharita (teaspoon). Diminutives have different endings, depending on the word concerned. Without going into the rules of grammar, (masculine) diminutive endings include:

~ecito	~ecillo	~ezuelo
~cito	~cillo	~zuelo
~ito	~illo	~uelo

Augmentative words, e.g. cuchara (spoon); cucharón (ladle) have different endings, including the following (masculine) ones:

| ~ón | ~azo (f ~aza or ~ada depending on meaning) |
| ~ote | ~achón | ~azo |

Sometimes diminutives and augmentatives are combined: silla (chair), sillón (armchair), silloncito (small armchair).

Abbreviations &c:
[Andes] = Andes
[Ar] = Argentina
[Asturias] = Asturias (N-W Spain)
[CAmer] = Central America
[Carib] = Caribbean (West Indies)
[Chile] = Chile
[Colom] = Colombia
[Cuba] = Cuba
[LatAm] = Latin America
[Mex] = Mexico
[Peru] = Peru
[RPlate] = River Plate
[SAm] = South America
[SCone] = Southern Cone (Argentina, Paraguay, Uruguay, Chile)
[Spain] = Spain
[Venez] = Venezuela

Spanish Cuisine

Spurred on by the prestige of obtaining the coveted *Michelin* Guide's star (rosette) rating restaurants in Spain itself have improved no end, and Spain has restaurants with each of the three Michelin ratings. As is to be expected, ingredients are influenced by the locality. They are also influenced by history, both ancient and modern. In Spain the Moorish influence is evident; in Peru, even the Japanese; in Patagonia, the Welsh and Scottish, with a strong Southern Cone preference for charcoal-grilled red meats and, along the coasts (Chile is all coast!), for local seafood, particularly molluscs and, more recently, for farmed sea fish.

Gastronomic Dictionary is designed to enable the diner to make sense of menus written in Spain and in other parts of the spanish-speaking world. It covers many of the questions a traveller might ask a waiter in a restaurant. It also enables the diner to select a restaurant by reading menus first, and choosing one according to what one fancies at the time. Several restaurants may be equally good, but according to one's mood, one menu may appeal more than another at any particular moment! *Gastronomic Dictionary* may also prove useful to the spanish-speaking waiters with english-speaking customers; and to cookery students.

The definitions are not intended to describe every aspect of a dish, but just enough of the basic ingredients to indicate its character; and it does not cover specialist restaurants (e.g. Chinese).

Gastronomic Dictionary also covers many kitchen implements and receptacles. This is because dishes are often described by the pots they are cooked in. For the same reason a few wines are included. And because travelling involves accommodation, a few hotel terms, car parking terms &c feature among the definitions.

Let us know what additions you can contribute (and in the same format with gender, applicable regions &c as in *Gastronomic Dictionary*).

¡Buen Provecho!
Enjoy your Meal!

A

abacado *nm* [Carib] avocado pear

abacería *nf* (of shop) grocery

abacero (a) *nm/f* grocer

abacora *nf* [LatAm] sea fish: tuna variety

abadejo *nm* sea fish: cod; ling; [Carib] sea fish: swordfish; dried salted cod

abalón *nm* mollusc: clam

abarrote (tienda de ~s) *nm* (of shop) grocery

abarrotería *nf* [LatAm] (of shop) grocery

abarrotero (a) *nm/f* [LatAm] grocer

abastecedor (a) *nm/f* [Mex] wholesale butcher

abastero *nm* [Mex, SCone] wholesale butcher

abasto *nm* [SCone] (of meat market) public; [Carib] (of shop) grocery; basic foodstuffs

ablandar *vt* to tenderise; (of guts) to loosen

abocado *a* (of wine) smooth, agreeable; (of sherry) medium-sweet

abocar *vt* to pour out; to decant

abrebotellas *nm* bottle-opener

abrelatas *nm* tin/can-opener

abridor *nm* bottle-opener; tin-opener

abril *nm* April

abrillantado *a* glazed; *nm* glaze

abrillantar *vt* to glaze

abrir *vt* to open; to cut; (of appetite) to whet

absorber *vt* to absorb

abstemio *a* teetotal; *nm/f* teetotaller

acalorado *a* hot, heated

acalorar *vt* to warm up; to heat up

acalórico *a* low-calorie

acaramelado *a* caramelized; over-sweet; (of flavour) toffee-flavoured

acaramelar *vt* to caramel

acecinar *vt* (of meat) to cure; to salt

acedar *vt* to make bitter; to turn sour

acedera *nf* sorrel

acedía *nf* acidity, sourness; sea

fish: plaice

acedo *a* acid, sour; sharp

aceite *nm* oil; ~ **de oliva** olive oil; ~ **de oliva virgen** virgin olive oil

aceitera *nf* oil bottle; ~**s** oil/vinegar cruet

aceituna *nf* olive; ~ **rellena** stuffed olive

aceitunado *a* olive

acelga *nf* swiss chard

acerbo *a* (of wine) off; sour; bitter

ácere *nm* maple

acha (hacha) *nf* sea fish: halfbeak

achampañado *a* champagne-flavoured

achicalado *a* [Mex] sugared

achicalar *vt* [Mex] to honey

achicharrar *vt* (of frying) to crisp

achicharronar *vt* [LatAm] to flatten, to crush

achicoria *nf* chicory, endive

achupalla *nf* [LatAm] pineapple

achura *nf* [SCone] offal

acidez *nf* sourness, acidity

acidillo *a* slightly sour

ácido *a* acid, sour; (of apple) cooking; **crema ~a** sour cream; ~ **salicílico** salicylic acid

aclarar *vt* (of wine &c) to clarify

acompañamiento *nm* accompaniment; side-dish; garnish

acompletadores *nmpl* [Mex] beans

acondicionado *a* (of air) conditioning; *nm* ~ **de aire** air-conditioner

acordeón *nm* accordion

acre *a* (of flavour/taste) bitter, sharp

acrimonia *nf* (of flavour/taste) sourness; sharpness

acuerdo *adv* (of taste/quantity) according to

acuosidad *nf* (of fruit) juiciness; succulence

acuoso *a* (of fruit) juicy; succulent

adelgazante *a* slimming; *nm* slimming-product

aderezar *vt* to prepare; to season; to garnish; to dress; (of drinks) to mix; (of wine) to blend

aderezo *nm* seasoning; dressing; preparation; garnish

adobado *nm* pickled pork; *a* (of meat) marinated

adobar *vt* to cook, to prepare, to dress; (of meat) to season, to pickle

adobera *nf* [SCone, Mex] (of cheese &c) brick-shaped; cheese mould

adobo *nm* preparation; pickle; sauce; [Mex] red chili sauce

adornar *vt* to garnish; (of dish) to decorate

adorno *nm* garnish; (of dish) decoration

afilado *a* sharp; tapering

afilador *nm* (of knife) sharpener

afrechillo *nm* [SCone] bran

afrecho *nm* bran

afrutado *a* fruity

agachadiza *nf* game bird: snipe

agalla *nf* (of fish) gill

ágape *nm* banquet

agarrar *vt* to stick; to stick to

agave *nf* agave; tequila-producing plant

agosto *nm* August

agrazón *nm* wild grape

agregado *nm* side-dish

agregar *vt* to add

agria *nm* ~ **crémor** cream of tartar; *a* [SCone] sour, sharp

agriado *a* [SCone] sour, sharp

agridulce *a* bitter-sweet; **cerdo** ~ (of pork) sweet and sour

agrifolio *nm* holly

agrio *a* sour, tart; *nm* **arándano** ~ cranberry; sour juice; ~**s** citrus fruits

agriura *nf* [LatAm] sourness, tartness

agrura *nf* sourness, tartness

agua *nf* water; ~ **con gas** (of mineral water) fizzy; ~ **sin gas** (of mineral water) still; ~ **blanda** soft water; ~ **de cebada** barley water; ~**s de consumo** drinking water; ~ **corriente** running water; ~ **dulce** fresh water; ~ **del grifo** tap-water; ~ **(de) panela** [Col, Venez] hot lemon; ~ **perra** [Chile] boiled water; ~ **de seltz** seltzer, soda water; ~ **mineral** mineral water; ~ **potable** drinking water; ~ **tónica** tonic water

aguacate *nm* avocado pear

aguacola *nf* [Mex] fish glue, isinglass

aguado *a* (of milk, wine) watered down, diluted; (of coffee) weak

aguaducho *nm* small alfresco café; soft-drinks kiosk

aguamiel *nf* honeyed/sugared water; [CAmer, Mex] fermented maguey (agave) juice

aguapié *nm* plonk

aguar *vt* (of wine) to water down; to dilute

aguardiente *nm* brandy, spirits; ~ **de caña** rum; ~ **de cerezas** cherry brandy; ~ **de manzana** applejack

aguaturma *nf* Jerusalem artichoke

aguinaldo *nm* Christmas box

agüita *nf* [Chile] herbal tea

aguja *nf* sea fish: garfish; marlin; [CAmer, Mex] beef; ~**s** shoulder, sparerib; (of wine) sparkling; savoury meat/fish pastry; dessert pastry

agujilla *nf* sea fish; South Pacific saury

ahogado *nm* [Andes] (of sauce/stew) tomatoes/peppers/onion-ed

ahuecar *vt* to hollow out

ahumado *a* smoked; (of whisky) smoky

ahumar *vt* to cure; to smoke

aire *nm* air; ~ **acondicionado** air-conditioning

aireado *nm* (of wine) aeration

ajarabezado *a* (of wine) syruped

ajedrea *nf* (of herb) savory

ajenjo *nm* (of drink) absinth(e); wormwood liqueur

ajerezado *a* sherried; sherry-flavoured

ajete *nm* young garlic

ají (**ajises** *pl*) *nm* [LatAm] chili (pepper); red pepper; (of sauce) chili

ají de color *nm* [Chile] paprika

ajiaceite *nm* (of sauce) garlic/olive oil

ajiaco *nm* (of stew) potato/chili; [Chile] pork/vegetable soup; spiced potato dish

ajilimoje *nm* (of sauce) garlic/pepper

ajilimójili *nm* (of sauce) garlic/pepper

ajillo *nm* chopped garlic; **al ~** garlic-accompanying/cooked; **gambas al ~** garlic prawns

ajiseco *nm* [Andes] red pepper

ajo *nm* garlic; **un ~** (of garlic) clove; (of sauce) garlic; **sal de ~** garlic salt

ajoaceite *nm* (of sauce) garlic/oil

ajoarriero *nm* cod/oil/garlic/peppers dish

ajoblanco *nm* (of cold soup) garlic/almond

ajonjolí *nm* sesame

ala *nf* wing

albacora *nf* sea fish: albacore; long-fin tunny; swordfish

albahaca *nf* (of herb) basil

albaricoque *nm* apricot

albariño *nm* Galician wine variety

albérchigo *nm* peach

albero *nm* tea cloth, dishcloth

albóndiga *nf* meatball

albondigón *nm* large meatball

albumen *nm* egg white

albur *nm* [Spain] freshwater fish: bleak

albura *nf* egg white

alcachofa *nf* artichoke

alcahué (cacahuete) *nm* peanut, monkey-nut, groundnut

álcali *nm* alkali

alcamonías *nfpl* (of seasoning) aromatic seeds

alcaparra *nf* caper

alcaparrón *nm* caper

alcaravea *nf* caraway

alcaucil *nm* [SCone] artichoke

alcayota *nf* squash, marrow

alcazuz *nm* liquorice

alce *nm* moose

alcohol *nm* alcohol

alcohólico *a* alcoholic; **no ~** (of drink) soft, non-alcoholic

alcorza *nf* icing sugar

alcorzar *vt* to ice

alcuza *nm* olive oil bottle; [LAm] oil/vinegar cruet

alcuzcuz *nm* couscous

alechado *a* [LatAm] milky

alemán *a* german

aleoyota *nf* [SCone] pumpkin

alergeno (alérgeno) *nm* allergen

aleta *nf* (of fish) fin

aleudar *vt* (of yeast) to leaven

alevín *nm* (of young fish) fry

alevino *nm* (of young fish) fry

alfajor *nm* [Spain] Christmas cake; [SCone] sweet filled biscuit; cake variety

alfandoque *nm* [LatAm] cheesecake; [Col, Peru] caramel bar

alfanje *nm* seafish: swordfish

alfeñique *nm* toffee paté

alforfón *nm* buckwheat

Alfredo *a* [Chile] (of pasta) ham/mushroom/cream/ parmesan-ed

alga *nf* seaweed

algarroba *nf* carob

algodón *nm* cotton

alhucema *nf* lavender

aliado *nm* [SCone] toasted sandwich; mixed drink

Alicante *nm* red wine

alimentación *nf* food, feeding; grocer's; ~ **natural** health food

alimentar *vt* to feed; *vti* to be nourishing/nutritious

alimentario *a* food

alimenticio *a* food; nutritive; nourishing

alimento *nm* food; ~**s naturales** health foods

alimentoso *a* nourishing

aliñar *vt* (of salad) to dress; (of stew) to season; to garnish

aliño *nm* (of salad) dressing; (of stew) seasoning; garnish

alioli *nm* aïoli; garlic mayonnaise

aljofifa *nf* floor-mop

alella *nm* spanish wine variety

almacén *nm* [LatAm] grocery

almansa *nm* spanish wine variety

almeja *nf* clam variety

almendra *nf* almond; kernel; (of almond) ~ **garapiñada** sugared almond; ~ **tostada** toasted almond; (of peach) stone

almendrada *nf* almond milk-shake

almendrado *a* (of flavour) nutty; *nm* macaroon

almíbar *nm* syrup

almibarado *a* syrupy, sugary; excessively sweet

almilla *nf* pork breast

almodrote *nm* (of sauce) cheese/garlic

almozar *vt* to lunch; to brunch

ampurdán *nm* spanish wine variety

almuerzo *nm* lunch; brunch; ~ **de negocias** business lunch; ~ **de trabajo** working lunch

alón *nm* (of fowl) wing

alondra *nf* lark

alquitara *nf* (of whisky) still

alrededor *adv* (of decoration &c) around

alterar *vi* (of food/milk &c) to go off

alubia *nf* kidney bean; **~ pinta** pinto bean

aluminio *nm* **papel de ~** cooking foil, kitchen foil, tin foil

alzar *vt* (of table/dishes) to clear

amalgamar *vt* to blend

amanezca *nf* breakfast

amanita *nf* mushroom variety: grisette

amaranto *nm* amaranth; chinese spinach

Amaretto *nm* Amaretto aperitif

amargar *vi* to be bitter, to taste bitter; *vt* to make bitter, to sour

amargo (amargoso [LatAm]) *a* (of flavour) bitter, tart; *nm* (of flavour) bitterness, tartness; [SCone] bitter tea, Paraguayan tea; **~s** (of drink) bitters

amargón *nm* dandelion

amargor *nm* (of flavour) bitterness, tartness

amarillo *nm* [Carib] ripe banana; *a* yellow

amarrar *vt* to tie up; to truss

amasamiento *nm* kneading

amasandería *nf* [Andes, SCone] bakery

amasandero (a) *nm/f* [Andes, SCone] baker

amasar *vt* (of flour &c) to knead; to mix

amasijo *nm* kneading; [Carib] bread

amastado *a* (of bread) home-kneaded

ambientado *a* [Mex] air-conditioned

ambigú *nm* buffet

ambrosía *nf* ambrosia; food for the gods

amelcocharse *vpr* [Mex] (of sugar) to set, to harden

América *nf* America

americano *a* (of coffee) large black; (of breakfast) with fruit juice/omelette &c

aminorar *vt* (of price) to cut

amoladura *nf* (of knife) sharpening; grinding

amoldado *a* moulded

amontillado *nm* amontillado, medium sherry

amortiguado *a* (of onion &c) made blander

anacardo *nm* cashew nut

ánade *nm* duck; **~ real** mallard; **~ silbón** widgeon, wigeon

anadón *nm* duckling

anafe *nm* portable cooker

analcohólico *a* (of drink) soft; non-alcoholic

ananá (ananás) *nm* pineapple; **ananasa** *nf* [Andes] pineapple

anaquel *nm* shelf

anca *nf* [Andes] toasted maize; **~ de rana** frogs' legs

ancho *a* broad; wide

anchoa *nf* anchovy; blue fish

anchoveta *nf* [Andes] anchovy

andaluz *a* Andalusian

andarica *nf* [Asturias] crab

angarillas *nfpl* cruet

angélica *nf* angelica

angelito *nm* angel-fish

angelote *nm* angel-fish

angostura *nf* angostura bitters

anguila *nf* eel

angula *nf* young eel, elver; sea fish: peladilla

anillo *nm* ring

animal *nm/a* animal

anís *nm* anise, aniseed; (of drink) anisette

anisado *a* aniseed-flavoured

anisete *nm* anisette, aniseed liqueur

anjova *nf* sea-fish: chad

anona *nf* [CAmer, Mex] scaly custard apple, sweetsop, sugar-apple

ánsar *nm* goose

ansarino *nm* gosling

anta *nf* moose

ante *nf* moose; [Mex] macaroon

antes *a/adv* before

antiácido *nm/a* antacid

antiadherente *a* non-stick

antialcohólico (a) *nm/f* teetotaller

anticolesterol *a* low-colesterol

anticucho *nm* [Peru, Chile] (of ox/calf hearts) spicy kebab

antieconómico *a* uneconomic

antojitos *nmpl* [SCone] sweets; [Mex] (of tapas) nibbles

antucá *nm* [SCone] sunshade

añada *nf* (of time) season

añadir *vt* to add

añejarse *vpr* (of wine) to age, to mature

añejo *a* (of wine, cheese) mature; (of ham) well-cured

apagar *vt* to turn off; (of thirst) to quench

apagavelas *nm* (of candle) snuffer; extinguisher

apanado *a* [LatAm] breadcrumb-ed

apanar *vt* [LatAm] to breadcrumb

apañado *nm* sea bass variety

aparacoches *nm/f* parking attendant

aparcadero *nm* car park

apaste (apaxte) *nm* [CAmer] earthenware jug

aperital *nm* [SCone] aperitif

aperitivo *nm* aperitif

apetecible *a* appetising; mouth-watering

apetito *nm* appetite

apetitoso *a* appetising

apí *nm* [Andes] non-alcoholic maize drink

apiado *nm* [SCone] celery liqueur

apio *nm* celery; ~ **nabo** celeriac

aporreado *nm* [Carib] (of stew) meat; chili stew

apoyado *a* (of lemon slice &c on rim of glass) placed

apretador (chitón) (quitón) *nm* mollusc variety

apropiado *a* suitable

aprovisionamiento *nm* (of food) stocking

apurar *vt* (of food/drink) finish-up; to hurry

árabe *a* (of bread) pitta

arándano *nm* blueberry, bilberry; ~ **agrio** (~ **colorado**) (~ **encarnado**) cranberry

arandela *nf* [Col] bun

arból *nm* tree

arce *nm* maple

ardilla *nf* squirrel

arenque *nm* herring; ~ **ahumado** kipper

arepa *nf* [LatAm] maize pancake; maize biscuit

arequipa *nf* [Andes] rice pudding

argolla *nf* ring

armadillo *nm* armadillo

armado *nf* freshwater fish: armado

arnero *nm* [LatAm] sieve

aro *nm* napkin ring

aroma *nm* aroma; (of wine) bouquet

aromático *a* aromatic

aromatizante *nm* aromatic spice; flavouring

aromatizar *vt* to spice; to herb

arrancharse *vpr* to eat together

arrayan *nm* myrtle

arrebañar *vt* to clear up; (of meal) to eat up

arrebatado *a* overcooked, burned

arrebozar *vt* to coat, to cover; (cup) to brim

arreglar *vt* (of salad) to dress; (of flowers) to arrange

arriba *adv* up; above

arribazón *nf* plethora of fish

arrocero *a* rice

arrollado *nm* [SCone] rolled pork

arrope *nm* syrup *(esp grape/honey)*

arroz *nm* rice; ~ **a la cubana** plantain/tomato sauced/fried egged rice; ~ **graneado** fried then boiled rice; ~ **hinchado** puffed rice; ~ **con leche** rice pudding; ~ **integral** brown rice

arrurruz *nm* arrowroot

artesiano *a* (of well) artesian

ártico *a* Arctic

artículo *nm* article; ~s **alimenticios** food; ~s **de plata** silverware

arveja *nf* [LatAm] pea; mange-tout; sugar pea

arvejado *nm* (of dish) with peas

arvejita *nf* [LatAm] small pea

asadera *nf* [SCone] baking tin

asadero *nm* spit roaster, oven; *a* roasting; [Mex] cottage cheese

asado *a* roast, roasted; *nm* roast; [LatAm] joint; barbecue [SCone] barbecued food; (of potato) roast; baked

asador *nm* spit; ~ **a rotación** (~ **rotatorio**) rotary spit; (of restaurant) carvery

asadura *nf* chitterlings; **~s** offal

asar *vt* to roast; **~ al horno** to bake in oven; **~ a la parrilla** to grill

ascender *vt* to go upstairs

ascensor *nm* lift; elevator

asentarse *vpr* to sit down

asentido *a* seated

aseos *nmpl* WC, toilet

asiento *nm* chair; seat; (of meat) sirloin cut; (of bottle base); sediment

asistir *vt* to attend

asomado *a* (of presentation) poking-out; showing

asperillo *nm* (of taste) slightly bitter/sour

áspero *a* sour, tart

aspirina *nf* aspirin

ástaco *nm* crayfish

asurar *vt* to burn

atado *nm* [LatAm] (of cigarettes) packet

atarugar *vt* to over-eat

ate *nm* [Mex] quince jelly

atecomate *nm* [Mex] tumbler

¡atención! *nf* warning!

atipujarse *vpr* [CAmer, Mex] to over-eat

atocinar *vt* [Ar] to cut up; (of meat) to cure

atol (atole) *nm* [LatAm] (of drink) cornflour

atóxico *a* non-poisonous

atún *nm* seafish: tuna

atunero *a* tuna

auge *nm* (of restaurant/ crowdedness &c) peak time

augmentar *vt* to add to; to increase

automático *nm* [SCone] self-service restaurant

automercado *nm* supermarket

autoservicio *nm* self-service restaurant

ave *nf* bird; chicken; **~ de corral** chicken, fowl; **~s de corral** poultry

avellana *nf* hazelnut; filbert

avena *nf* oats

averiado *a* (of fruit &c) bruised

avestruz *nm* ostrich

avícola *a* poultry

avinagrado *a* (of flavour) acid; sour

avisador *nm* timer

avisar *vt* (of taxis &c) to call

aviso *nm* notice

avutarda *nf* bustard; large game bird

ayanque *nm* Peruvian weakfish

ayer *adv* yesterday

ayote *nm* [Mex, CAmer] pumpkin

ayotoste *nm* armadillo

ayuya *nf* [SCone] scone, roll

azafrán *nm* saffron

azafranado *a* (of flavour/ colour) saffroned

azafranar *vt* to saffron

azúcar *nm/f* sugar; **~ blanco(a) (~ blanquillo (a))** white sugar; **~ Demerara (rubia [Chile])** demerara; brown sugar; **~ granulado (a)** granulated; **~ moreno (a) (~ negro (a))** brown sugar; **~**

flor, (~ en polvo [Colom]) **(~ impalpable** [Arg]) icing sugar; **~ lustre** caster sugar; **~ terrón (~ cortadillo)** lump sugar; **~ de caña** cane sugar
azucarado *a* sweet, sugared
azucarar *vt* to sugar; (of cake) to ice; to sweeten
azucarero *nm* sugar bowl; *a* sugar
azul *a* (of cheese *esp*) blue
azulejo *nm* [Mex] blue shark
azulina *nf* cornflour
azumbre *nm* gallon

B

baba *nf* [Col, Ven] small crocodile
babaco *nm* papaya variety
babador *nm* bib
babero *nm* bib
bacaladero *a* cod
bacaladillo *nm* sea fish: whiting variety
bacalao *nm* sea fish: cod; wreckfish; [Chile] Patagonian toothfish
bacanal *a* bacchanalian
bachicha *nf* [Mex] dregs
bacón *nm* bacon
bagazo *nm* mash of sugar cane
bagre *nm* [LatAm] catfish; **~ amarillo** yellow catfish; **~ blanco** white catfish
baho *nm* [CAmer] meat/yucca dish
bailador (a) *nm/f* dancer

bailaor (a) *nm/f* dancer; flamenco dancer
bailar *vt* to dance
bailarín (a) *nm/f* dancer; **~ de claqué** tap-dancer
baile *nm* dancing
bajativo *nm* [SCone] digestif
balanza *nf* (of kitchen) scales
ballena *nf* whale
balón (copa) *nm* [Ar] brandy balloon
bambú *nm* bamboo
banana *nf* banana
banano *nm* [LAm] banana
banasta *nf* hamper
banco *nm* (of fish) shoal
bandeja *nf* tray; (of cheese) board; (of fruit/vegetables &c) (in a) tray/pack
banderilla *nm* canapé; small kebab; appetizer
bangaña *nf* gourd, calabash
banquete *nm* banquet; **~ de boda** wedding feast; **~ de gala** state banquet
bantam *nf* bantam
bañar *vt* to soak; to cover; to immerse
baño *nm* (of food) covering; soaking; immersion; (of facilities) toilet, WC
baño maría *nm* bain-marie; double boiling-pan
bar *nm* bar
bar-restaurante *nm* bar-restaurant
barato *a* cheap
barbacoa *nf* barbecue; [CAmer,

Mex, Venez] (of meat) barbecued; [Andes] kitchen-rack

barbo *nm* freshwater fish: barbel; ~ **de mar** sea fish: red mullet

barbón *nm* goat

barbuno *nm* mullet

bardana *nf* (of herb) burdock

barman *nm* barman

barquillo *nm* (of ice-cream) cornet, cone; rolled wafer

barra *nf* (of chocolate) bar; (of bread) stick; loaf

barracuda *nf* barracuda

barrica *nf* large barrel

barriga *nf* [Chile] stomach

barril *nm* barrel

barrilete *nm* cask; sea-fish: mackerel tuna; skipjack tuna

barro *nm* earthenware; [Chile] ~**s jarpa** (of toasted sandwich) cheese/ham; **(~s luca)** (of toasted sandwich) cheese/meat

base *nf* bed; base layer of food

basmati (arroz) *nm* long thin-grained rice

bastante *a* enough

bastoncito *nm* (of bread) stick

bastonera *nf* umbrella-stand

bastonero (a) *nm/f* compère

batata *nf* yam, sweet potato

batería *nf* ~ **de cocina** kitchen equipment

batido *nm* batter; milk shake; ~ **de frutas** fruit shake; *a* **crema** ~**a** (of cream) whipped

batidor *nm* whisk; ~ **mecánico** egg-whisk; [CAmer] wooden mixing bowl

batidora *nf* (of food) mixer, blender; whisk; ~ **de brazo** hand-blender

batir *vt* (of eggs) to beat; to whisk; (of cream) to whip; (of milk) to churn; (of batter) to cream

bauco *nm* black sea chub

bautizar *vt* (of liquid) to dilute

bavaroise (bavarois) *nm* flavoured rich custard

baya *nf* berry; ~ **del saúco** elderberry; ~ **de enebro** juniper berry

bayeta *nf* (of cleaning) cloth

bayo *nm* [Mex] bean

bayunca *nf* [CAmer] bar

bebedero *a* drinkable

bebedizo *a* drinkable

beber *vt* to drink

beberaje *nm* [SCone] *(usu alcohol)* drink

bebestible *a* [LatAm] drinkable

bebestibles *nmpl* drinks

bebezón *nf* [Carib] drinks

bebible *a* drinkable

bebida *nf* drink; ~ **no alcohólica,** ~ **refrescante** soft drink

becacina *nf* snipe

becado (a) *nm/f* woodcock

bechamel *nf* béchamel sauce

beicon *nm* bacon

bejín *nm* puffball

bejuquillo *nm* [Andes] vanilla

belleto *nm* acorn fed pig

bellota de mar *nf* sea urchin
bendecir la mesa *vt* to say grace
bendición de la mesa *nf* grace
benjamín *nm* half-bottle
berberecho *nm* cockle
berdel *nm* mackerel
berenjena (berengena) *nm* aubergine, eggplant
berlina (berline *nm* [Chile]) *nf* [SCone] doughnut
berro *nm* watercress
berza *nf* cabbage; ~ **lombarda** red cabbage
besamel *nf* béchamel sauce; white sauce
besugo *nm* sea fish: sea bream; cardinal fish
besuguera *nf* fish kettle; sea fish: bream
betabel *nm* beetroot
betarraga *nf* [LatAm] beetroot
betarrata *n* beetroot
betún *nm* [Mex, Chile] topping; icing
bicarbonatado *a* fizzy
bicarbonato *nm* baking powder
bicha *nf* [Andes] large cooking pot; snake
biche *a* unripe; *nm* [Andes] large cooking pot
bicho *nm* [Andes] snake
bidel *nm* bidet
bien *adv* well; *nm* good
¡bienvenido! *excl* welcome!
bierzo *nm* spanish wine variety
bife *nm* steak; fillet; [SCone] beefsteak
bífidus *nm* (of live yogurt) bifidus
biftec *nm* steak
bígaro (bigarro) *nm* winkle; seawater snail
bilagay (breca) *nm* sea-fish: morwong
bimbollo *nm* [Mex] bun
binissalem *nm* spanish wine variety
bioagricultura *nf* organic agriculture
biodegradable *a* biodegradable
biogénesis *nf* biogenesis
biologico *a* organic
birra *nf* beer
birrí *nm* [Andes] snake
birria *nf* [Mex] stew; [Spain] pork stew; [CAmer] beer
birutilla *nf* [SCone] abrasive
biscote *nm* rusk
bisonte *nm* bison
bisté (bistec) *nm* steak
bíter *nm* bitters
bivalvo *nm/f* (of mollusc) bivalve
bizcochera *nf* biscuit tin
bizcocho *nm* sponge cake, finger; [Mex] biscuit; [LatAm] digestive biscuit; ~ **borracho** wine/syrup-soaked sponge cake
blanca *a* (of bean) haricot
blanco *a* white; ~ **y negro** creamed iced coffee; *nm* (of egg) white

blando *a* (of water) soft; (of paste) smooth; (of meat) tender; [SCone] (of meat) white

blandorro *a* bland, tasteless

blandura *nf* (of meat) tenderness; (of water, paste) softness

blanquear *vt* to blanch

blanquillo *a* white; [CAmer] egg; [Chile, Peru] white peach; [Carib, SCone] whitefish; southern sandperch

blanquín *nm* [Carib] (of chicken) egg

Bloody Mary *nm* Bloody Mary, vodka/tomato juice cocktail

boca *nf* mouth; ~ **de mar** crab stick; (of wine) flavour; (of crab &c) pincer

bocadillería *nf* [Spain] sandwich/snack bar

bocadillo *nm* [Spain] (of french bread) sandwich; [Chile] cocktail tit-bit

bocadito *nm* morsel; [Andes] ~**s** snack, appetizer

bocado *nm* mouthful; canapé

bocadulce *nf* sea-fish: houndshark

bocal *nm* jar

bocanada *nf* (of drink) swig

bocaracá *nm* [CAmer] snake

bocarte *nm* anchovy

boche *nm* [Chile] chaff

bock *nm* beer glass

bocoy *nm* (of port) hogshead

boda *nf* (of reception) wedding; **pastel de** ~ wedding cake

bodega *nf* (of wines &c) cellar

bodegón *nm* inexpensive restaurant

bodeguero (a) *nm/f* wine producer

boga *nf* freshwater fish: boga

bogavante *nm* lobster

bol *nm* bowl; (of wine &c) punchbowl; [LatAm] fingerbowl

bola *nf* (of cheese) Edam; (of dough &c) ball; (of ice-cream) scoop

boletus *nm* boletus mushroom

boliche *nm* [SCone] café

bolillo *nm* rolling-pin; [Mex] bread roll

bolita *nf* small ball

bollería *nm* pastries; patisserie

bollero (a) *nm/f* pastry chef

bollo *nm* bread roll; bun

boloñesa *nf* (of sauce) bolognese

bolsa *nf* packet; bag; pack; ~ **de asar** roasting bag

bolsita *nf* tea-bag

bombilla *nf* drinking straw; [SCone] maté filtered drinking straw

bombo *a* [Mex] (of meat) off, bad; [Cuba] tasteless

bombón *nm* chocolate

boniato *nm* [Carib] yucca, cassava; sweet potato; yam

bonito *nm* sea fish: tuna, bonito

boquerón *nm* sea fish: anchovy

boquilla *nf* (of cigarette) holder
borbón *nm* bourbon
borbotar *vi* to boil over
bordalesa *nf* [SCone] large
  wine barrel
borde *nm* (of glass &c) rim
borgoña *nm* (of wine)
  burgundy
bori bori *nm* meat balls/maize/
  vegetables/cream cheese
  stew
borona *nf* maize; [CAmer] crumb
borra *nf* young ewe
borracho *a* alcohol-soaked; (of
  cake) tipsy; (of fruit) marinated
borraja *nf* borage
borrego (a) *nm/f* lamb; sheep
borrico (a) *nm/f* donkey
bosque *nm* forest
bota *nf* barrel; wineskin
botana *nf* [Mex] appetizer
botar *vt* [Ven, Colom, Chile] to
  remove; to swill out
bote *nm* jar; container; (of
  drinks) can
botella *nf* bottle
botellero *nm* wine-rack
botellín *nm* small bottle; half
  bottle
botijo (a) *nm/f* earthenware jug
botijuela *nf* earthenware jug
botillería *nf* [Chile] off-licence
botiquín *nm* [Carib] drinks
  cupboard/cabinet; first-aid kit
boto *nm* wineskin
botones *nm* bellboy
boutifar *nm* spiced sausage
boutique del pan *nf* specialist

bakery
bóveda *nf* cellar
bovino *a* bovine
boyé *nm* [SCone] snake
braille *nm* braille
brandada *nf* cod/potato/garlic/
  milk purée
brandy *nm* brandy
brasa *nf* (of meat) grilled on
  barbecue
braseado *a* spit-roast
brasería *nf* grill
brasero *nm* [Mex] small cooker
bravo *a* [LatAm] spicy; hot
brazo *nm* foreleg; ~ **de gitano**
  [SCone ~ **de reina**] swiss roll
brazuelo *nm* (of meat) shoulder
breca *nf* freshwater fish: bleak
brécol *nm* broccoli
bren *nm* bran
bretones *nmpl* brussels
  sprouts
breva *nf* flat cigar; [Carib] (of
  cigar) good quality
brindar *vt* (cheers!) to toast
brindis *nm* (of welcome) toast;
  [Andes, Carib] cocktail party
británico *a* (of breakfast)
  english
brocha *nf* [SCone] skewer
brocheta (broqueta) *nf*
  skewer; kebab; brochette
broculí (bróculi) (brócoli) *nm*
  broccoli
brote *nm* shoot; ~**s de soja**
  bean shoots
brótula *nf* [Chile] sea-fish:
  tadpole mora

Bruselas *nfpl* (of sprouts) brussels

brut *a* (of sparkling wine) very dry, brut

budín *nm* pudding; (of fish) pie; [LatAm] cake

budinera *nf* [SCone] pudding bowl; mould; steamer

buccino *nm* whelk

buchada *nf* (of liquid) mouthful

buche *nm* (of liquid) mouthful

bueno (buen) *a* good; large

buey *nm* ox; ~ **de francia** crab; ~ **de mar** crab/crayfish variety

bufé (buffet) (bufet) *nm* buffet; restaurant; dining-room

bufeo *nm* [CAmer, Carib, Mex] sea fish: tunny

bujía *nf* candle; candlestick

bule *nm* gourd; squash

bullabesa *nf* bouillabaisse; fish soup

bullas *nm* spanish wine variety

buñuelo *nm* fritter

buqué *nm* (of wine) bouquet

burbujeante *a* (of drink) fizzy

burdeos *nm* (of wine) claret, Bordeaux

burgos *nm* soft creamy cheese

burro *nm* donkey

buseca *nf* [SCone] stew

butifarra *nf* blood sausage; [Peru] meat/salad roll

C

caballa *nf* sea-fish: mackerel;

[SCone] chub mackerel

caballo *nm* horse

cabecita *nf* (of asparagus &c) tip

cabello de ángel *nm* sweet pumpkin filling; ~**s de ángel** pasta vermicelli

cabeza *nf* head; stick; (of garlic) onion; [LatAm] (of bananas) bunch; ~ **de jabalí** ([Chile] **queso de ~)** brawn

cabezón *a* (of wine) heady

cabillo *nm* (of plant) stalk

cabina *nf* (of telephone) box, kiosk, booth

cabinza *nf* sea-fish: cabinza grunt

cabra *nf* goat; (of cheese) goat cheese; ~ **montés** (of goat) ibex

cabracho *nm* scorpion fish

cabrahígo *nm* wild fig

cabrales *nm* Roquefort-type cheese

cabrerizo *a* goat

cabrilla *nf* sea-fish: rockfish; ~ **chileno** banded sea bass

cabritas *nfpl* [Chile] popcorn

cabrito *nm* kid; young goat

cacahuete (cacahuate) *nm* peanut; monkey-nut; ground-nut

cacao *nm* cocoa

cacerola *nf* casserole dish; saucepan

cachalote *nm* sperm whale

cacharrería *nf* crockery

cacharro *nm* pot

cachaza *nf* rum-like liqueur

cachejo *nm* [Spain] (of bread) morsel

cachete *nm* [CAmer] flavour

cachetear *vt* [SCone] to eat well

cachivache *nm* pot

cacho *nm* crumb, small piece; (of bananas) hand; freshwater fish: chub; sea fish: red surmullet; ~ **de cabra** hot chili variety

cachucho *nm* sea fish: bream

cachuela *nf* rabbit or pork offal stew

cacillo *nm* ladle

cactus (cacto) *nm* cactus

cada *a* each

caesar *a* (of salad) caesar; lettuce/vinaigrette/raw egg/ Worcestershire sauce salad

café *nm* coffee; ~ ~ real coffee; ~ **americano** large black coffee; ~ **cerrero** strong black coffee; ~ **completo** continental breakfast coffee; ~ **con leche** white coffee; ~ **cortado** coffee with a splash of milk; ~ **descafeinado** decaffeinated coffee; ~ **en grano** coffee beans; ~ **espreso** espresso coffee; ~ **instantáneo (~ soluble)** instant coffee, soluble coffee; ~ **molido** ground coffee; ~ **natural** lightly-roasted coffee; ~ **negro** high roasted coffee; [Chile] ~ **puro (~ tinto)** black coffee; ~ **solo** black coffee; ~ **torrefacto (~ tostado)** roasted coffee

café-concierto *nm* live music café

café-teatro *nm* café with theatre

cafecito *nm* [LatAm] black coffee

cafeína *nf* caffeine

cafetalero *a* [LatAm] coffee

cafetera *nf* coffee maker/ machine; coffee pot; ~ **automática** coffee machine; ~ **de filtro** filter coffee

cafetería *nf* café; cafeteria; coffee shop; (on trains) buffet/refreshment car; coffee retailer

cafetero/a *nf* café owner

cafetín *nm* small café

caipiriña *nf* Brazilian sugar-cane cocktail

caja *nf* cash desk; checkout; till; seed shell; carton; box

cajeta *nf* [LatAm] fudge; [Mex] caramel topping; jelly; [CAmer, Mex] sweet

cajete *nm* WC; toilet

cajetilla de cigarrillos (~ de tabaco) *nf* packet of cigarettes

caju *nm* cashew nut

cala *nf* (of fruit) sample slice; taster

calabacín *nm* courgette

calabacita *nf* [Spain] courgette

calabaza *nf* pumpkin; gourd;

squash; marrow; calabash

calabazo *nm* pumpkin, gourd, squash, marrow, calabash

calafate *nm* [SCone] barberry

calaguasca *nf* [LatAm] rum

calamaco *nm* [Mex] kidney bean

calamar *nm* squid

calatayud *nm* spanish wine variety

cálamo *nm* (of plant) stalk

calcio *nm* calcium

caldera *nf* [SCone] teapot; kettle

caldereta *nf* (of shellfish/lamb) ragoût; stewpan

calderón *nm* cauldron

caldillo *nm* [Chile] soup

caldo *nm* soup; broth, consommé; (of stew) juice; liquid; **cubitos de ~** stock cubes; (of sherry) wine; oil; [Mex] sugar cane juice; **~ de carne** beef tea

caldoso *a* runny, watery

calentar *vt* to heat up; to warm

calidad *nf* quality

cálido *a* hot

calientafuentes *nm* hotplate

caliente *a* hot

calimocho *nm* wine/cola drink

caliqueño *nm* cheap cigar

callampa *nf* [Chile] mushroom

callana *nf* [LatAm] flat earthenware dish

calle *nf* road; street

callos (cayos) *nmpl* tripe

caloría *nf* calorie

calorífugo *a* ovenproof

caluga *nf* [SCone] toffee

Calvados *nm* Calvados, cider brandy

calzones rotos *nmpl* [SCone] doughnuts

camarero (a) *nm/f* waiter (waitress); **~ principal** maître d'hôtel; head waiter; (on ship) steward (stewardess)

camarón *nm* shrimp

cámbaro *nm* crayfish

cambucho *nm* [SCone] (of ice-cream) cone

cambur *nm* banana

camomila *nf* camomile (chamomile)

camote *nm* [LatAm] sweet potato, yam

campaña *nf* countryside

campechana *nf* [Carib, Mex] cocktail; [Mex] seafood cocktail

campestre *a* wild

campo *nm* field; country; [Andes] farm; **~ de borja** spanish wine variety

camuesa *nf* (of apple) pippin

canalones *nmpl* cannelloni

canapé *nm* canapé

canasta *nf* basket

canastillo *nm* small wicker basket

canastito *nm* small basket

canasto *nm* hamper

cancha *nf* [LatAm] toasted maize

canchar *vt* to toast

canco *nm* [SCone] pottery jug

cande *a* (of confectionery) sugar candy

candeal *nm* [SCone] egg flip; *a* (of bread) white bread

candela *nf* candle; candlestick

candelero *nm* candlestick

candi *a* (of sugar) rock candy

candiota *nf* wine cask

caneca *nf* spouted wine bottle; [Mex] earthenware pot; [Andes] tin, can

canela *nf* cinnamon

canelones *nmpl* cannelloni; meat or cheese or seasonings-filled pasta

caneton *nm* (of dish) primarily duck

cangrejo *nm* seafood: crab; (of river) crayfish; **pata de ~** crabstick

canguro (a) *nm/f* kangaroo

canilla *nf* shank; shin; (of poultry) wing bone

cantalupo *nm* ([CAmer] **~a** *nf*) cantaloupe; musk-melon

cántara *nf* jug

cantidad *nf* quantity

cantimplora *nf* hip-flask

cantina *nf* buffet, refreshment car, bar; trattoria; wine cellar; hamper; [Andes] milk churn

canto *nm* (of table &c) edge; (of bread) crust

canutillo *nm* pasta variety: small tubes

canutos *nmpl* pasta variety: tubes

caña *nf* cane; stalk; small glass

of beer; cane spirit; (of sugar) cane; (of meat) shank; [LatAm] (of drink) straw

cañamiel *nf* sugar cane

cañazo *nm* [Andes] cane liquor

cañita *nf* [Andes] (of drink) straw

caño *nm* wine cellar

capa *nf* (of cake) layer

capachito *nm* small wicker basket

capacidad *nf* capacity

caparazón *nm* shell; nose-bag

capear *vt* to cover, to top

capi *nf* [SCone] maize; maize flour

capia *nf* [SCone] maize flour

capitán *nm* [Mex] head waiter

capón *nm* capon, fattened young cock; mutton

cápsula *nf* bottle-top

capuchina *nf* nasturtium

capuchino *nm* (of coffee) cappuccino; frothed milk-topped coffee

caqui *nm* [SCone] date plum

carabao *nm* far-eastern buffalo

carabinero *nm* prawn

caracol *nm* snail; **~ de mar** winkle

caracoles *nmpl* pasta variety: shells

carajillo *nm* brandied/liqueured coffee

caramel *nm* sardine

caramelizado *a* caramelized

caramelo *nm* sweet; caramel; **a punto de ~** caramelized

caraota *nf* bean
carbohidrato *nm* carbohydrate
carbón *nm* coal; **~ de leña (~ vegetal)** charcoal
carbonada *nf* [Andes, SCone] meat stew; (of meat) steak, chop; [SCone] (of soup) thick soup, broth; (of meat) mince; **~ criolla** stew stewed in pumpkin; onioned/beer-ed meat stew
carbonatado *a* fizzy
carbonato de calcio *nm* calcium carbonate
carboncillo *nm* charcoal
cardamomo *nm* (of herb) cardamom
carey *nm* turtle
cargado *a* (of coffee/alcohol &c) strong
cargazón *nf* (of fruit tree) heavy crop
caribú *nm* caribou; N American reindeer
cariñena *nm* spanish wine variety
carioca *a* from Rio de Janeiro
carlota *nf* charlotte; (of mixed fruit) baked in bread-lined mould
carmenère *nm* Chilean wine variety
carne *nf* meat; **~ en gelatina** brawn; **~ de membrillo** quince jelly
carnero *nm* mutton
cárnico *a* meat
carnitas *nfpl* [Mex] barbecued pork
carnoso *a* meaty
caro *a* expensive
carolina *a* (of pudding) brandy/coconut/chocolate/milk/biscuit dessert
caroya *nm* sweet white wine
carozo *nm* (of maize) cob
carpa *nf* freshwater fish: carp
carpaccio *nm* Italian appetizer; very thin-cut raw lemon-ed meat/fish
carpeta *nf* table cover
carral *nm* barrel
carrillo *nm* cheek
carrito *nm* [Carib] taxi; **~ de postres** dessert trolley
carro comedor *nm* [Mex] dining/restaurant car
carta *nf* menu; **a la ~** à la carte; **~ de vinos** wine list
carterita de fósforos *nf* book of matches
cartílago *nm* cartilage
cartón *nm* box; carton; container; pack
casa (de comidas) *nf* cheap restaurant; **de la ~** home-made; (of wine) house
casabe *nm* cassava bread
casado *nm* [LatAm] (of dish) two separate foods
casca *nf* grape spirit; marc
cascanueces *nm* nutcracker
cascar *vt* (of egg) to break; (of nut) to crack
cáscara *nf* (of fruit) skin; peel; rind; (of nut/egg) shell

cascarón *nm* eggshell

casco *nm* (of fruit) piece; segment; slice

cáseo *nm* curd

caseoso *a* cheesy

casero *a* home-made

casilla *nf* [Andes] WC, toilet

casino *nm* [SCone] canteen

casis *nm* blackcurrant; cassis; **~ de rojo** redcurrant

caspiroleta *nf* [Andes, Carib, SCone] egg-flip

casquería *nf* tripe/offal shop

casquinona *nf* [Andes] beer bottle; beer

castaña *nf* chestnut; nut; **~ de agua** water chestnut; **~ de Brasil** Brazil nut; **~ de cajú (caju)** cashew nut

castañetas *nfpl* castanets

castaño *a* chestnut

castañuela *nf* castanet; demijohn

castellano *a* of Castile

cata *nm/f* (of food/wine) tasting, sampling; **~ de vino** wine-tasting

catabre *nm* [Carib, Andes] gourd

catalán (ana) *a* Catalan, Catalonian; (of cream) crème brûlé

catar *vt* to taste; to sample

catavinos *nm* (of person) wine-taster; (of cup) tastevin, tâte-vin

catsup *nm* ketchup

causa *nf* [SCone] snack; [Peru] cold fish/potato pie

causear *vi* [Chile] to snack

causeo *nm* [Chile] tomato/onion/cold-meat dish

cava *nf* (of wine) cellar; sparkling champagne-method wine matured in cellar; [Carib] icebox

caviar *nm* caviar(e)

cayena *nf* cayenne pepper

caza *nf* (of hunting) game

cazabe *nm* cassava bread/flour

cazo *nm* saucepan; ladle

cazoleta *nf* small pan

cazón *nm* sea fish: dogfish; tope shark

cazuela *nf* casserole-dish; (of meat) stew, casserole

cebada *nf* barley; **~ perlada** pearl barley; **agua de ~** barley-water

cebado *a* (of animal) fattened-up

cebar *vt* (of maté) to brew

cebiche (seviche) *nm* [SCone] (of hors d'oeuvre) sauced raw fish/shellfish

cebolla *nf* onion; **~ escalonia** shallot

cebollado *a* [LatAm] onions-cooked

cebollana *nf* chive

cebolleta *nf* spring onion, scallion; chive

cebollino (a) *nm/f* spring onion, scallion; chive

cebollita china *nf* spring onion

cebón *nm* fattened-up animal

cebú *nm* zebu; ox

cecina *nf* smoked/cured meat; [Chile] pork sausage

cedazo *nm* sieve

cedrón *nm* [SCone] lemon verbena

cele *a* (of fruit) unripe

celebrar *vt* to celebrate

celeque *a* unripe, green

celestino *nm* [SCone] hot manjar pancake

cemita *nf* [LatAm] white bread roll

cena *nf* supper; dinner; main meal; ~ **de gala** banquet; ~ **de trabajo** working meal; ~ **espectáculo** floor-show dinner

cena-bufete *nf* buffet-supper

cenaduría *nf* [Mex] restaurant

cenar *vt* to dine

cenceño *a* (of bread) unleavened

cenicero *nm* ashtray

centeno *nm* rye

centolla *nf* king crab

centollo (a) *nm/f* spider crab; [Chile] king crab

centollón *nm* [Chile] king crab

cepillar *vt* (of shellfish &c) to scrub

cera *nf* [Andes, Mex] candle; ~**s** honeycomb

cerafolio *nm* chervil

cerceta *nf* (of duck) teal

cerdito (a) *nm/f* piglet

cerdo *nm* pig; pork; ~ **marino** porpoise

cereales *nmpl* (of breakfast) cereals

cereza *nf* cherry

cerillo *nm* [esp CAmer] match

cerneja *nf* fetlock

cerner (cernir) *vt* to sieve

cernido *nm* sifting; sifted flour

cernidor *nm* sieve

cernidura *nf* sifting

cerrado *a* closed

cerrar *vt* to seal

cerrado *a* (of restaurant/shop) closed

cerrarse *vi* (of shop) to close

cerrero *a* (of animal) wild; [LatAm] unsweetened; bitter

cerval *a* deer

cervatillo *nm* fawn

cervato *nm* fawn

cervecería *nf* bar; pub

cervecero *a* beer

cerveza *nf* beer; lager; **caña de** ~ glass of beer; ~ **de barril** draught beer; ~ **negra** stout; ~ **rubia** lager

cesta *nf* steamer

cesto (a) *nm/f* hamper

cetácio *a* cetacean; of whales

ceviche *nm* [Andes] (of fish) small coriander/onion/lemon-raw dice

chabacano *nm* [Mex] apricot

chacalín (a) *nm/f* shrimp

chacarera (a la) *a* [Chile] (of tomato) egg/sweetcorn/onion-stuffed

chacarero *nm* [Chile] sandwich

chachacaste *nm* [CAmer]

brandy

chacina *nf* pork; cold meats

chacinero *a* pork

chacolí *nm* Basque wine variety; [Chile] new wine

chafalote *nm* freshwater fish: tiger characin

chafar *vt* (of potato &c) to mash

chagual *nm* [Chile] bromelia (pineapple-like) fruit

chalona *nf* [LAmer] dried meat

chalote *nm* shallot

chalupa *nf* [Mex] filled maize-cake

chamorro *nm* (of pork) leg

champán *nm* champagne

champanero *a* champagne

champaña *nm* champagne

champañero *a* champagne

champiñón (champi) *nm* mushroom; **crema de ~** cream of mushroom soup

champun(e)ar *vt* to mix a cocktail

champurrado *nm* [LAmer] cocktail; [Mex] chocolate drink

champurreado *nm* [SCone] pot-luck dish

chancaca *nf* [CAmer] maize cake ; [LAmer] brown sugar

chánchamo *nm* highly-seasoned maize/meat dish; tamale

chancharro *nm* scorpion fish

chanchito *nm* [Chile] sucking pig

chancho (cha) *nm/f* [LatAmer] pig/sow; **carne de ~** pork

chanco *nm* [Chile] hard cow's milk cheese variety

chanfaina (xanfaina) *nf* onions/peppers/vegetables sauce; budget stew

changurro *nm* crab

chanquetes *nmpl* whitebait

chapo *nm* [Mex] maize porridge

chapsui *nm* chopsuey

chara *nf* young rhea

charadrio *nm* plover

charal *nm* [Mex] small fish

charape *nm* [Mex] agave drink

charcutería *nf* assiette anglaise; delicatessen

charquecillo *nm* [Andes] dried fish; [SCone] dried vegetables/fruit

charqui *nm* [LatAm] jerked beef; [SCone] (of fruit/vegetable/meat) dried

charquicán *nm* [SCone] dried vegetable/meat dish

chascar *vt* to swallow

chato *nm* tumbler

chaucha *nf* [SCone] green bean, string bean; [Peru] food

chauchau *nm* stew

chaufa *nf* [LatAm] fried rice

chayote *nm* chayote; choco

chef *nm* chef

chembo *nm* [Andes] slab of meat

chibola *nf* [CAmer] fizzy drink

chicha *nf* [LatAm] maize spirit; grape juice

chícharo *nm* [LatAm] pea; chickpea

chicharra *nf* [CAmer, Carib] (of pork) crackling

chicharro *nm* sea fish: horse-mackerel

chicharrones de cerdo *nm* pork scratching

chichería *nf* [Andes] chicha bar; maize liquor bar

chichicaste *nm* [CAmer] nettle

chico *a* small

chicoria *nf* chicory

chicote *nm* cigar

chifa *nf* [Peru, Chile] chinese restaurant

chilacayote *nm* chilacayote, gourd-variety

chilaquiles *nmpl* [Mex] chile/tomato-fried tortilla

chilcano *nm* [Peru] (of drink) cherry-brandy/pisco/cola

chile *nm* chili (pepper); **~ con carne** chili con carne

chilena (a la) *a* (of stewed pork) spiced onion/carrot/garlic/celery-garnished

chilindrina *nf* [Mex] sugar-topped bun

chilindrón (al) *nm* tomatoes/peppers-cooked or sauced

chilote *nm* [LatAm] baby sweetcorn

chiltoma *nf* [CAmer] sweet pepper

chimbo *nm* [Chile] slab

chimichurri *nm* [SCone] spicy barbecue sauce

chimpín *nm* [Andes] brandy

china *nf* china; [Carib, Mex] (of fruit) orange; *a* (of sauce) soya; **cebollita ~** spring onion

chinchibí *nm* [Andes, CAmer, SCone] ginger beer

chinchibirra *nf* [SCone] ginger beer

chinchón *nm* aniseed spirits

chinchona *nf* quinine

chinguirito *nm* [Mex, Carib] eau-de-vie

chino *nm* [CAmer, Andes] pig

chip *nm* crisp

chipirón *nm* young squid

chiquito *nm* (of wine) small glass; *a* small

chirimoya *nf* custard apple

chiringuito *nm* (of sustenance) stall

chirivía *nf* parsnip

chirla *nf* mussel; baby clam

chisporrotear *vi* to sizzle

chitón (quitón) (apretador) *nm* mollusc variety

chiva *nf* (of goat) kid

chivito *nm* [Urug] steakburger; **~ canadiense** (of sandwich) meat/egg/salad

chivo *nm* goat

chocha *nf* mollusc: Pacific trochita

chocha perdiz *nf* woodcock

chocho *nm* (of confectionery) stick; **~s** sweets; **~ de altramuz (~ de vieja)** lupin seed

choclo *nm* sweetcorn

choco *nm* cuttlefish

chocolate (choco) *nm*

chocolate; cocoa; drinking chocolate; ~ **blanco (con leche)** milk chocolate; ~ **negro** plain chocolate; **crema de ~** chocolate filling; ~ **de algarroba** carob

chocolatería nf chocolate café

chocolatero a chocolate; nm [Andes] chocolate pot

chocolatín nm [RPlate] chocolate bar

chocolatina nf chocolate bar

cholga nf [SCone] mussel variety

chompipe (chumpipe) nm [CAmer] turkey

chongo nm [Mex] bun

chonta nf [Andes] palm shoots

chop nf [Chile] lager/beer glass; draught beer

chopería nf [Chile] beer bar

chopito nm young squid

chorcha nf (of fowl) comb

choricillo nm frankfurter-like sausage

choripan nm [SCone] crisp-bread spicy hot-dog

chorito nm Chilean mussel

chorizo nm spicy hard pork sausage; [SCone] rump steak

chorlito nm plover

choro nm [Andes] mussel variety; [SCone] ~ **zapato** very large mussel variety

chorote nm [Mex, Venez, Andes] drinking chocolate; [Carib] (of drink) watery, dilute; coffee; [Andes] chocolate pot

chorrear vt (of liquid) to pour

chorrillana (a la) a [Chile] (of fried egg) fried tomato/onions/garlic/coriander-accompanied

chorrito nm drop

chorro nm (of water &c) jet

chuchería nf (of confectionery) sweet; titbit

chucho nm custard centred doughnut; a (of fruit) soft

chuchoca nm [Chile] maize flour

chucrut nm sauerkraut

chufa nf tiger nut; **horchata de ~** tiger nut drink

chuflay nm [SCone] punch

chuico nm demijohn

chulengo nm young guanaco

chuleta nf (of meat) chop, cutlet

chuletada nf barbecue

chuletón nm T-bone steak

chumbera nf prickly pear

chumbo nm prickly pear

chumpipe (chompipe) nm [CAmer] turkey

chunchules nm [Chile] intestines

chuño nm [LatAm] potato starch

chupe nm [Andes, SCone] stew; [SCone] snack; tapa

chupete [LatAm] ([Col] **chupeta** nf) nm lollipop

chupetín nm [RPlate] lollipop

chupín nm [Ar] fish/potato stew

chupón nm lollipop; ~ **de caramelo** toffee apple

churdón nm raspberry; (of raspberry) syrup

churrasco nm barbecued meat; [SCone] steak

churrasquear vi [SCone] to eat steak

churrasquería nf [SCone] steak-house

churro nm fried dough strip (accompanying coffee/hot chocolate)

churumbela nf [CAmer] maté cup

chusco nm (of bread) crust

ciboulette nf chive

cidra nf citron

cidracayote nm [LatAm] calabash, gourd

cidro nm citron

ciervo nm venison

cigala nf Dublin Bay prawn; crayfish, crawfish

cigales nm spanish wine variety

cigalita nf small crayfish

cigarrería nf [LatAm] tobacconist's

cigarrillo nm cigarette

cigarro nm cigarette; ~ **puro** cigar; ~ **habano** Havana cigar

cilantro nm (of herb) coriander

cilindro nm cylinder

cimarrón (rrona) a wild; [SCone] (of maté) unsweetened

cinchona nf [LAmer] quinine bark

cinco a five

cinta nf (of pork) loin; ribbon; nfpl ~**s** pasta: tagliatelle

ciruela nf (of fruit) plum; ~ **claudia (~ verdal)** greenage;

~ **damascena** damson; ~ **pasa (~ seca)** prune; ~**s pasas en tocino sobre pan tostado** devils on horseback

cisne nm swan

cítrico a citric

cítricos nmpl citrus fruits

citrón nm lemon

cívico nm [Ar] large beer

clara nf egg white; [Spain] shandy

clarea nf cinnamoned/sugared/spiced white wine

clarete nm red wine; claret

clarificación nf (of wine/spirits) clarification

claro a (of tea/coffee) weak, dilute; (of soup) thin; nm [Carib] guava jelly; sugar cane spirits

claudia nf greengage

clavillo nm clove

clavo (~ de olor) nm clove; ~ **oxidado** whisky/Drambuie® digestif

clementina nf clementine, tangerine

clericó nm [SCone] mulled wine

cliente (a) nm/f customer

clientela nf clientele

climatización nf air-conditioning

climatizado a air-conditioned

climatizador nm air-conditioner

cloaca nf drain

coagulación nf (of milk &c) curdling

coagular vt (of milk &c) to

curdle

cobertera *nf* cover, lid

cobre *nm* copper pans

coca *nf* Coke®, Coca-Cola®

cocada *nf* [CAmer] coconut sweet

cocción *nf* cooking; ~ **al horno** baking; ~ **al vapor** steaming

cocer *vt* to cook, to boil; *vi* (of wine) to ferment

cochayuyo *nm* [LatAm] seaweed

coche *nm* car; ~ **comedor (~-restaurante)** dining/restaurant-car; [Mex] taxi; [CAmer, Mex] pork; pig

cochecito *nm* wheelchair

cochemonte *nm* [CAmer] wild boar

cochinilla *nf* cochineal

cochinillo *nm* suck(l)ing pig

cochino *nm* pig, hog; ~ **de leche** suck(l)ing pig

cochura *nf* (of cakes &c) batch

cocido *a* boiled, cooked; **bien ~** well done; *nm* [Spain] (of meat/bacon/chickpeas) stew; (of dish) pot-au-feu

cocina *nf* kitchen; cooker, stove; cookery, cooking, cuisine

cocinado *nm* cooking

cocinar *vt* to cook

cocinero (a) *nm/f* cook; ~ **jefe (a)** chef; sea-fish: kingfish

cocineta *nf* [Mex] kitchenette

cocinilla *nf* kitchenette; (of equipment) small cooker; chafing dish

coco *nm* coconut

cocoa *nf* cocoa

cococha *nf* fleshy part of cod/hake jaw

cocodrilo *nm* crocodile

cocol *nm* [Mex] sesame seed bun

cóctel *nm* cocktail; cocktail party

coctelera *nf* cocktail-shaker

código postal *nm* post-code

codillo *nm* knuckle; [Mex] pig's trotter

codorniz *nf* quail

cogedero *a* (of fruit) ready to pick; ripe

coger *vt* (of fruit) to pick

cogollo *nm* (of lettuce &c) heart; shoot; sprout

cohombro *nm* cucumber

coime *nm* [Andes] waiter

cojinoba (cojinova) *nf* sea-fish: palm ruff

col *nf* cabbage, ~ **china** Chinese leaves; ~ **de bruselas** brussels sprout; ~ **lombarda** red cabbage ~ **de Saboya** savoy cabbage; ~ **rizada** curly kale, collard; ~ **roja** red cabbage

cola *nf* (of drink) cola, Coke®; [Andes] fizzy drink; ~ **de naranja** orangeade; ~ **de pescado (colapís) (colapiz)** isinglass; ~ **de mono** [Chile] milk/coffee/vanilla rum punch; tail

colación *nf* light meal; [LatAm]

box of sweets

coladera *nf* strainer

coladero *nm* colander; sieve; (of tea &c) strainer

colador *nm* colander; sieve; (of tea &c) strainer

coladuras *nfpl* (of coffee &c) grounds; dregs

colágeno *nm* collagen

colapís (colapiz) (cola de pescado) *nm* isinglass; fish glue

colar *vt* to strain

colesterol *nm* cholesterol

colicuar *vt* to dissolve, to melt

coliflor *nf/m* cauliflower; ~ **con queso** cauliflower cheese

colín *nm* breadstick

colinabo *nm* kohlrabi

coliqüe *nm* [Arg, Chile] bamboo

colita *nf* tail

colmado *nm* (of restaurant) economy seafood; (of teaspoon &c) heaped

colmena *nf* beehive; [Mex] bee

colocar *vt* (of ingredients) to stand; to place

colorado *a* (of bean) ~**a** runner; **arándano** ~ cranberry

colorante *nm* colouring

colorear *vi* (of fruit) to ripen

colza *nf* colza, rape; (of oil) rape-seed

combinado *nm* cocktail

comedero *nm* dining-room; road-side café; *a* edible

comedor *nm* restaurant; dining-room

comer *vt* to eat; to lunch

comestible *a* eatable; edible

comida *nf* food; meal; lunch; [LatAm] dinner; ~ **basura (~ rápida)** fast food; ~ **corrida** set-price menu; ~ **de negocios** business lunch; ~ **preparada** pre-cooked; ~ **de trabajo** working lunch

comido *a* lunched

comino *nm* cumin

cómodo *a* comfortable

complemento *nm* complement; accompaniment

completa *a* (of milk) full-cream; *nf* [Carib] economy complete meal

completo *a* (of diet) balanced; (of restaurant) fully booked; (of hotel/B&B &c) no vacancies [SCone] **café ~** continental coffee; *nm* hot dog with trimmings

componente *nm* ingredient

componer *vt* to prepare

compota *nf* compote; fruit dish; preserve; (of pears &c) stewed

compotera *nf* dessert dish

comprar *vt* to buy

comprimido *nm* (of saccharine &c) tablet

conca de barberá *nf* spanish wine variety

concentrado *a* concentrated; *nm* extract, concentrate; ~ **de carne** meat extract

concha *nf* shell

concha de barberá *nm* spanish wine variety

concho *nm* taxi

condensado *a* (of milk) condensed

condimentación *nf* seasoning

condimentar *vt* to season; to flavour; to spice

condimento *nm* seasoning, flavouring; dressing

conejo *nm* rabbit; ~ **estirado** rabbit stew; *a* [CAmer] unsweetened; bitter; sour

confeccionar *vt* to bake; to make

confitado *a* crystallized

confitar *vt* to crystallize

confite *nm* sweet

confitería *nf* confectionery; sweet shop; [Andes, SCone] café/patisserie

confitura *nf* crystallized fruit; jam

congelado *a* frozen; chilled

congelador *nm* icebox; freezer

congeladora *nf* deep-freeze, freezer

congelar *vt* to freeze

congelarse *vpr* to freeze

congrio *nm* conger, conger eel; [Chile] ~ **dorado** pink cusk eel

Cono Sur *nm* Southern Cone (Chile/Argentine/Paraguay/Uruguay)

conserva *nf* jam; pickle; preserve; tin of; **en** ~ tinned

conservación *nf* preservation

conservador *a* preservative

conservante *nm* preservative

conservar *vt* to preserve

consomé *nm* consommé

consumición *nf* food; drink; ~ **mínima** minimum charge

consumido *a* (of fruit) dried-out

consumir *vt* to eat; to drink; to consume

consumirse *vpr* to boil off; to reduce

consumo *nm* **aguas de** ~ (of water) drinking

contáiner *nm* container

contante *a* (of money) cash

continental *a* (of breakfast) continental

continente *nm* container

convite *nm* banquet; invitation

convoy *nm* [Carib] salad; cruet

coñac *nm* cognac, brandy

copa *nf* glass; drink; (of pudding) cup; (of egg) boiled egg; ~ **balón** brandy balloon; ~ **flauta** (of glass) flute

copazo *nm* mixed alcohol/soft-drink

copeado *a* (of wine &c) sold by the glass

copero *nm* [SCone] waiter

copetín *nm* [Cuba, SCone] aperitif

copichuela *nf* drink

copita *nf* sherry glass

copos de *nmpl* (of oats) oatmeal; (of maize) cornflakes

coquilla *nf* [SCone] shell

coquina *nf* clam variety

coral *nm* (of lobster/crab) coral

coraza *nf* shell

corazón *nm* (of artichoke/ animal) heart; (of apple) core; (of fowl) breast

corbata *nf* (of pasta) bow

corbatita *nfpl* (of pasta) small bow

corcho *nm* cork

corcholata *nf* [Mex] crown cork

cordero (a) *nm/f* lamb

cordial *nm* cordial

cordillerano *a* [SCone] Andean

cordón *nm* [Andes, Carib] brandy; spirits

corégono *nm* whitefish

coriando *nm* coriander

corintos *nmpl* raisin variety

cornalina *nf* cornelian, dogwood cherry

cornflakes (cornflaques) *nmpl* [LatAm] cornflakes

coronado *nm* sea-fish: albacore; ~ **de** *a* crowned with

corral *nm* (of fowl) farmyard

correoso *a* (of meat) tough

corrido *a* (of meal) set-price

corriente *a* (of wine) ordinary, quaffing; (of water) running

corruptible *a* (of food) perishable

cortada *nf* (of bread) slice

cortadillo *nm* small glass; sugarlump

cortado *nm* coffee with a splash of milk; (of milk &c) *a* off; cut

cortahuevos *nm* egg-slicer; multi-bladed knife; mandolin

cortante *nm* cleaver

cortapuros *nm* cigar cutter

cortar *vt* to cut; to slice; to chop; (of mayonnaise/sauce &c) to curdle, to separate; (of milk &c) to go off, to curdle

corte *nm* cut; (of ice-cream) wafer

corteza *nf* (of bread) crust; (of fruit) skin, peel; (of cheese/ bacon) rind

corto *nm* (of beer, wine) small glass; (of coffee) black coffee; *a* (of ration) small

corvejón *nm* knuckle

corvina *nf* sea fish: sea-bass; southern grunt; ~ **negra** black drum; ~ **rubia** white croaker

corvinilla (huaiquil) *nf* sea-fish: drum

corzo *nm* (of male deer) roebuck

cos francesa (~ orejona [Mex]) *a* (of lettuce) cos

cosmestible *a* edible; ~**s** *nmpl* foodstuffs; groceries

costa brava *nm* costa brava

costers del segre *nm* spanish wine variety

costilla *nf* spare-rib; (of pork) chop; cutlet

costillar *nm* ribs

costra *nf* crust

costroso *a* crusty

cotufa *nf* Jerusalem artichoke; ~**s** *nfpl* [LatAm] popcorn

couscous (cuscús) (cuscus) *nm* couscous; broth-ed crushed wheat with meat/fruit; farinaceous stew

covín *nm* [SCone] popcorn

cozido *nm* chorizo/pig's-ears/ vegetable stew

crema *nf* cream; cream liqueur; ~ **ácida (~ agria)** sour cream; ~ **batida** whipped cream; ~ **de cacahuete** peanut butter; ~ **catalana** crème brûlé; ~ **chantilli (~ chantilly)** flavoured whipped cream; ~ **líquida** single cream; ~ **de champiñones** (of soup) cream of mushroom; ~ **de cacao (~ de chocolate)** chocolate filling; ~ **doble** double cream; **galleta de ~** custard cream; ~ **inglesa** custard; ~ **de limón** lemon curd; ~ **pastelera** pâtisserie cream; **queso ~** [LatAm] cream cheese

crémor tártaro *nm* cream of tartar

cremosidad *nf* creaminess

cremoso *a* creamy

crep (crepe) *nm* crêpe, pancake; **crepa** *nf* [LatAm] crêpe, pancake

crepería *nf* pancake restaurant, crêperie

crepitación *nf* (of frying) sizzling

crespa (uva) *a* gooseberry

crespo *a* (of parsley &c) curly

cresta *nf* cockscomb

criadilla *nf* testicle; potato; **~s de tierra** truffles; (of bread) small loaf, roll

crianza *nf* (of wine) vintage; **vino de ~** vintage wine

criar *vi* (of wine) to age, to mature

criba *nf* sieve

cribar *vt* to sift, to sieve

criollo *a* creole

crispetas *nfpl* [Andes] popcorn

cristal *nm* glass; crystal

cristalería *nf* glassware; set of glasses

crocante *a* crunchy; *nm* almond/caramel sweet; nutty chocolated ice-cream

croissan (croissant) (cruasán) *nm* croissant

croqueta *nf* croquette; deep fried breaded meat/fish balls; ~ **de pescado** fishcake

crostón *nm* crouton

cruasán (croissant) (croissant) *nm* croissant

cruce *nm* (of breeding) cross

crudeza *nf* (of meat) rawness; (of fruit) greenness, unripeness; (of water) hardness

crudo *a* raw; underdone; uncooked

crujiente *a* crunchy; crusty

crujir *vi* (of crackling &c) to crunch

crustáceo *nm* crustacean

crutón *nm* croûton

cuadrito *nm* cube; **cortar en ~s** to dice

cuajada *nf* junket, curd; cottage cheese; curd cheese

cuajado *a* (of milk) curdled; *nm* lemon curd

cuajaleche *nm* cheese rennet

cuajar *vt/vi* (of milk) to curdle; (of scrambled eggs) to set

cuajarse *vpr* (of milk) to curdle

cuajo *nm* rennet

cualidad *nf* quality

cuartelero *nm* [Andes] waiter

cuatro *a* four; quarter

cuba *nf* (of wine) barrel

cubalibre (cuba-libre) *nm* (of cocktail) white rum and Coke®; (of gin) gin and Coke®

cubano *a* Cuban

cubero *nm* cooper

cubertería *nf* cutlery

cubeta *nf* ice tray; cask

cubetera *nf* ice tray

cubierta *nf* topping, covering

cubierto *a* covered; topped; *nm* a piece of cutlery

cubilete *nm* cup; mould

cubitera *nf* ice-tray

cubito *nm* ice cube; **~ de caldo** stock cube

cubremesa *nf* tablecloth

cubretetera *nm* tea cosy

cubrir *vt* to cover; to top; to permeate

cucas *nfpl* sweets

cuchara *nf* spoon; **~ de café** teaspoon/coffee spoon; **~ de palo** wooden spoon,

cucharada *nf* spoonful; **~ rasa (~ rasada)** level teaspoonful; **~ de café** teaspoonful; **~ de sopa (~ sopera)** tablespoonful

cucharadita *nf* teaspoonful

cucharear *vt* to ladle out

cucharetear *vt* to stir

cucharilla *nf* (of tea/coffee) teaspoon

cucharita *nf* (of tea/coffee) teaspoon

cucharón *nm* ladle

cuche *nm* [CAmer] pig

cuchi *nm* pig

cuchilla *nf* kitchen knife; cleaver

cuchillería *nf* cutlery

cuchillo *nm* knife; **~ de carne** steak knife; **~ de pan (~ del pan)** bread knife; **~ de trinchar** carving knife

cuculí *nm* [Andes, SCone] woodpigeon

cucurucho *nm* ice-cream cornet

cuello *nm* (of bottle) neck

cuenco *nm* bowl

cuenta *nf* bill

cuerna *nf* drinking horn

cuerno *nm* croissant, roll; **~ de abundancia** horn of plenty

cuero *nm* skin; wineskin

cuerpo *nm* (of wine) body

cuesco *nm* (of olive &c) stone

cuete *nm* [Mex] stewing steak

cueva *nf* wine cellar

¡cuidado! *excl* care! warning!

culantro *nm* coriander

culebra *nf* snake; [Andes] bill

culén *nm* [Chile] basil variety herb

culengue *nm* mollusc: clam variety

culín *nm* (of liquid) drop

culinario *a* culinary

cultivo *nm* crop

cumpleaños *nm* birthday; **pastel de ~ (tarta de ~)** birthday cake

cuncho *nm* (of wine) dregs; (of coffee) grounds

cuñete *nm* keg

cupaje *nm* (of wine) blending

cúpula *nf* shell, husk

curaçao (curasao) *nm* orange-based liqueur

curadillo *nm* dried cod

curado *a* cured; *nm* curing

curanto *nm* [Chile] meat/seafood/vegetables (on) hot stones-cooked dish

curry *nm* curry

curso *nm* (of cookery classes) course

cuscha *nf* [CAmer] rum; spirits

cuscurrante *a* crisp, crunchy

cuscurro *nm* crouton (croûton); crust

cuscús *nm* couscous

cususa *nm* [CAmer] home-made spirits

cuya *nf* [SCone] gourd

D

dadito *nm* small dice

daiquiri (daiquirí) *nm* daiquiri; rum-based cocktail

damajuana *nf* demijohn

damasco *nm* damson; [SAm] apricot

damesana *nf* [LatAm] demijohn

danta *nf* moose

dátil *nm* date

debajo *adv* under

deber *vt* to owe

decantar *vt* (of wine) to decant

decocción *nf* reduction; thickening

decorado *a* decorated

dedo *nm* finger

deglutir *vt* to swallow

degollar *vt* (of animal) to slaughter

degustación *nf* (of wine &c) tasting, sampling

degustar *vt* to taste, to sample

dehuesado *a* (of meat) boned; (of fruit) stoned; (of olive) pitted, stoned

dehuesar *vt* (of meat) to bone, (of fruit) to stone, (of olive) to pit, to stone

dejar *vt* to allow to; to leave to

dejo *nm* aftertaste

delantal *nm* apron

delgado *a* (of slice) thin

delicia *nf* delight; delicacy

delicioso *a* (of food/drink) delicious

demasiado *adv* too much; excessive

denominación *nf* name; **~ de origen** (of wine &c) origin/

quality guarantee

dentado *a* (of knife) serrated

dente *nm* (of firmness) crunchy

dentro *adv* in; inside

derramar *vt* (of liquid) to spill

derredor *nm* proximity

derretido *a* melted

derretir *vt* to melt; to thaw

desaborido *a* tasteless

desabrido *a* tasteless

desaguar *vt* (of liquid) to drain-off

desalar *vt* to de-salt

desayunarse *vi* to breakfast

desayuno *nm* breakfast; ~ **a la inglesa (~ británico)** English breakfast; ~ **continental** continental breakfast; ~ **de trabajo** working breakfast; **cereales para el** ~ breakfast cereals

desazón *nf* tastelessness

desbordarse *vpr* (of liquid) to overflow

descafeinado *a* (of coffee) decaffeinated; *nm* decaffeinated coffee

descamisar *vt* (of fruit) to peel

descañonar *vt* (of poultry) to pluck

descapachar *vt* (of corn &c) to husk

descapsulador *nm* bottle-opener

descarnar *vt* to bone

descarozado *a* [SCone] (of fruit) dried

descascar *vt* (of egg) to shell; (of fruit) to peel

descascarar *vt* (of egg) to shell; (of fruit) to peel

deschalado *a* (of grain) husked

descomponerse *vi* to rot

desconchar *vt* (of shellfish) to de-shell

descongelado *a* defrosted

descorchador *nm* corkscrew

descortezar *vt* (of fruit) to peel

descremado *a* (of milk &c) low-fat, skimmed

descuartizar *vt* (of animal) to cut up

descuento *nm* discount

desear *vt* (of menu item) to desire; to want

desecado *a* (of fruit) dried

desgana *nf* lack of appetite

desganado *a* un-hungry

desengrasado *a* fat-free

desengrasar *vt* to skim off fat

desespinar *vt* to bone; to fillet

desgajar *vt* (of orange) to segment

desgranar *vt* to shell, to pod; (of grapes/maize &c) to remove individual fruit

desgrasado *a* fat-free

deshacerse *vpr* to melt; to dissolve; to crumble

deshecho *a* ruined; (of liquid) dissolved

deshelar *vt* (of fridge) to de-frost

deshilachado *a* [CAmer, Mex]

(of meat) stewed

deshojar *vt* (of fruit) to peel; [LatAm] to husk

deshollejar *vt* (of fruit) to skin; to peel

deshuesado *a* (of meat) boned; (of fruit) stoned; (of olive) stoned, pitted

desincrustar *vt* (of kettle) to de-scale

desmenuzable *a* crumbly, flaky; shredded

desmenuzar *vt* to crumble; to flake; to shred

desmoldar *vt* to remove from mould

desnatada (of milk) skimmed

desocupado *a* free; vacant; unoccupied; available

despacharse *vpr* to serve oneself

(d)espachurrar *vt* to flatten; (of fruit) to crush

despancar *vt* (of fruit) to husk

desparramar *vt* (of liquid) to spill

despegar *vt* to unstick

despellejar *vt* (of animal) to skin

despensa *nf* larder, pantry; provisions

despepitar *vt* to de-pip

desperdicios *nmpl* scraps; (of meat &c) non-eatable parts

desplumar *vt* (of fowl) to pluck

despojos *nmpl* (of animal) offal; (of meal) left-overs

despresar *vt* [SCone] (of fowl)

to joint

despuntado *a* (of knife) blunt

destapador *nm* [LatAm] bottle opener

destapar *vt* to open; to uncork; to remove lid

destilación *nf* distillation

destornillador *nm* screwdriver, vodka/orange cocktail

destripar *vt* to gut

desvede *nm* end of close season; game season start

devolución *nf* refund

devorador *a* (of hunger) ravenous

dextrosa *nf* dextrose; grape sugar

día *nm* day; del ~ (of milk/fish &c) fresh; ~ **festivo (~ feriada) (~ de fiesta)** public holiday; ~ **de vigilia** day of abstinence

diabético *a* diabetic

dibujo *nm* (of pastry) pattern; decoration; design

diciembre *nm* December

diente *nm* tooth; ~ **de ajo** garlic clove; ~ **de león** dandelion

dieta *nf* diet; [Andes] stew

dietético *a* **restaurante ~** restaurant for people on a diet; **alimento ~** diet food

diez *a* ten; tenth

diezmillo *nm* [Mex] sirloin

digerir *vt* to digest

digestivo *nm* digestif; post-prandial liqueur/spirits

digüeñes (dihueñe) (dihueñi) nm [Chile] mushroom: indian's bread (cyttaria)

Dijon nm **mostaza de ~** french mustard

diluido a (of tea, coffee) weak; diluted

dinero nm money

dirección nf address

discapacitado a/nm disabled

discreción nf a ~ according to taste

discrecional a (of ingredient) optional

disfrutar vt/vi (of meal) to enjoy

disminuir vt (of temperature) to lower

disolverse vpr to dissolve

dispendioso a expensive

disponer vt to set out

distilación nf distillation

dita nf [Carib] cup, dish

doblar vt to fold over

doble a double; (of coffee/ whisky/portion &c) large; **~ crema** [Mex] double cream

docena nf dozen; **media ~** half-dozen

domingo nm/adv Sunday

dona nf [LatAm] doughnut

donut nm doughnut

doña maria a bread roll variety

dorada nf gilthead bream

doradito a golden brown

dorado nm freshwater fish: dorado; dolphin fish; a (of potato) sliced/baked

dorar vt to brown

dos a two

dosificar vt to measure out

dosis nf (of saccharine &c) amount; quantity; dose

dragoncillo nm tarragon

Drambuie® nm Drambuie, scotch whisky-based liqueur

drogui nm [SCone] liquor

dromeo nm emu

dueño (a) nm/f proprietor (tress); host(ess)

dulce a sweet; **agua ~** fresh water

dulce nm sweet; **~ de almíbar** fruit in syrup; **~ de leche** [Ar] caramelized condensed milk; **~ de dulce** [SCone] flavoured condensed milk; [Chile, RPlate] jam; **~ de membrillo** quince jelly; **~s** patisseries, gateaux; [CAmer, Andes] brown sugar, sugar; [Andes] lollipop; a **agua ~** (of fish) freshwater

dulcificante nm sweetener

dulcificar vt to sweeten

dulzón (dulzarrón) a too sweet

dulzor nm sweetness

dulzura nf sweetness

durazno nm [esp. LatAm] peach

durezo nf (of water) hardness

duro a hard; (of meat) tough; (of bread &c) stale; (of fruit) unripe

E

ebullición nf boiling

echar *vt* (of drink) to pour; (of butter &c) to spread; (of salt &c) to add

económico *a* cheap, inexpensive

edible *a* [LatAm] edible

edulcoración *nf* sweetening

edulcorante *nm* sweetener

edulcorar *vt* to sweeten

efectivo *nm* cash

efervescencia *nf* fizziness

efervescente *a* fizzy

eglefino *nm* haddock

eider *nm* eider duck

ejote *nm* (CAmer, Mex) string bean

elaboración *nf* (of bread &c) baking; (of wine &c) production; **de ~ casera** home-made

electrodoméstico *nm* electrical appliance

elegante *a* (of restaurant &c) chic, smart; fashionable

elote *nm* [CAmer, Mex] corn on the cob

embeber *vt* (of biscuit &c) to soak

embocadura *nf* (of wine &c) flavour

embotellado *a* bottled

embotellar *vt* to bottle

embriagador *a* (of wine) heady

embuchado *nm* sausage

embuchar *vt* to stuff with mincemeat

embudo *nm* funnel

embutido *nm* sausage; **~s** delicatessen

empalagar *vi* to be sickly sweet

empanada *nm* empanada, pasty, pie; deep-fried filled pastry nibble

empanadilla *nf* small pasty, small pie; tuna/meat pasty

empanadita *nf* small empanada; small pasty; small pastry-case nibble

empanado *a* breadcrumb-ed; pastried

empanar *vt* to cook in pastry; to cook in breadcrumbs

emparedado *nm* sandwich

empella *nf* [LatAm] lard

emperador *nm* swordfish

empolvado *a* powdery

emú *nm* emu

encabezado *a* (of wine) fortified

encarnado *a* red; **arándano ~** cranberry

encebollado *a* onions-cooked

encendedor *nm* cigarette lighter

encentar *vt* (of loaf) to cut first slice of

enchilada *nf* [CAmer, Mex] meat or cheese stuffed chili-ed tortilla

enchilado *a* [CAmer, Mex] chili-ed; *nm* [CAmer, Mex] chili-ed stew

enchilar *vt* [LatAm] to chili

enchiloso *a* [CAmer, Mex] hot-tasting

encima *adv* on top

encimera *nf* (of kitchen) hob; worktop

encomendero *nm* [Peru] grocer; [Carib] meat wholesaler

encorchar *vt* (of bottle) to cork

encurtidos *nmpl* pickles

encurtir *vt* to pickle

endibia (endivia) *nf* endive; chicory

endrina *nf* sloe

endrino *nm* sloe

endulzante *nm* sweetener

endulzar *vt* to sweeten

endurecer *vt* (of butter &c) to harden

enebro *nm* juniper

eneldo *nm* dill

energético *a* (of drink &c) stimulating; invigorating

enero *nm* January

enfrascar *vt* to bottle

enfriadero *nm* cold-store

enfriamiento *nm* refrigeration

enfriar *vt* to cool; to chill

engordante *a* fattening

engordar *vt* (of animal) to fatten-up

enguagar *vt* to rinse out

enharinar *vt* to flour

enjundia *nf* (of animal) fat

enlardar *vt* to baste

enlatado *a* tinned; canned

enlozado *a* enamelled

enmantecar *vt* to butter; to grease

enmantequillar *vt* to butter; to grease

enófilo (~a) *nm/f* wine expert

enólogo (~a) *nm/f* wine expert

enoteca *nf* (of wine) cellar; wine in cellar

enrejillado *nm* steamer mesh/grille

enriquecido *a* enriched

ensaimada *nf* (of bread) snail shaped bun

ensalada *nf* salad; **~ de col** cole-slaw; **~ de fruta** fruit-salad

ensaladera *nf* salad bowl

ensaladilla *nf* (of salad) diced vegetable; **~ rusa** Russian salad

ensartador *nm* [SCone] roasting spit

ensartar *vt* (of meat) to spit-roast

ensopar *vt* to dunk

entendido (a) *nm/f* connoisseur

entera *a* (of milk) full-fat

entero *a* whole; (of potato) jacket

entibiar *vt* (of liquid) to cool; to reduce to tepid

entonelar *vt* to en-cask

entrada *nf* entrance; foyer; (of menu) starter

entrante *nm* starter

entraña *nf* (of meat) fillet rib cut; **~s** entrails

entrecot (entrecó) *nm* entrecôte; sirloin steak

entremés *nm* side-dish;
  entremeses hors d'oeuvres;
  (of hors d'oeuvres) **~ salado**
  savoury
entremesera *nf* hors
  d'oeuvres platter
entremeses *nmpl* hors
  d'oeuvres; light first dish to
  meal
entrepriso *nm* [LatAm]
  mezzanine
entresuelo *nm* mezzanine
entreverado *a* (of bacon)
  streaky
envasado *nm* (of liquids)
  bottling; canning
envase *nm* bottle; can, tin,
  container; **~s a devolver**
  returnable empties
envejecer *vt* (of wine) to age;
  to mature
envuelto *a* wrapped
enzima *nf* enzyme
epazote *nm* [Mex] herb tea
epicúreo (a) *nm/f* epicurean
equino *nm* horse; sea urchin
equipaje *nm* luggage
equipar *vt* to equip
erizo *nm* hedgehog; **~ de mar**
  (**~ marino**) sea urchin
ermitaño (a) *nm/f* hermit crab
escabechada *nf* stew
escabechado *nm* marinating;
  pickling
escabechar *vt* to pickle
escabeche *nm* (of sauce)
  pickle, brine; (of small fish)
  soused fish

escaldar *vt* to blanch
escalera *nf* stairs
escalfador *nm* chafing dish
escalfar *vt* (of egg) to poach
escalonia (cebolla) *nf* shallot
escalopa *nf* [Chile] escalope,
  cutlet
escalope *nm* escalope, cutlet;
  ~ de ternera escalope of
  veal
escalopín *nm* fillet
escama *nf* (of fish) scales
escamar *vt* (of fish) to de-scale
escamoso *a* (of fish) scaly
escanciador (a) *nm/f* wine
  waiter, sommelier
escanciar *vt* (of wine) to pour
escaparse *vpi* (of liquid) to leak
  out
escaramujo *nm* rosehip
escarbadientes *nm* toothpick
escarbajas *nfpl* firewood
escarchado *a* (of fruit)
  crystallized
escarchar *vt* (of cake) to ice;
  (of fruit) to crystallize
escarcho *nm* sea fish: gurnard
escarola *nf* escarole, curly
  endive; chicory
escasez *nf* scarcity
escobilla *nf* brush; **~ de
  dientes** toothbrush
escobillar *vt* [Chile] (of shellfish
  &c) to scrub
escocés *nm* (of whisky)
  Scotch; **~ de malta** malt
  whisky
escombro *nm* mackerel

escón *nm* scone

escone *nm* scone

escorpena (escorpina) *nf* scorpion fish

escote (pagar a) *nm* to go dutch

escribano *nf* sea-fish: halfbleak

escualo *nm* dogfish

escudilla *nf* bowl

escuedella *nf* vegetables/meat/pasta/stuffed-turkey dish

escupidera *nf* spittoon

escurreplatos *nm* plate-rack

escurrido *a* (of liquid) strained

escurridor *nm* plate-rack; colander

escurrir *vt* (of liquid) to drain; to drip; to strain

escurrirse *vi* (of liquid) to drip

esencia *nf* essence

esmerejón *nm* sea-fish: merlin

esmoquin *nm* dinner jacket

espachurrar *vt* to flatten; (of fruit) to crush

espada *nf* **(espadarte** *nm*) sea-fish: swordfish

espadín *nm* (of small fish) sprat

espaguetis *nmpl* spaghetti

espalda *nf* back

espaldilla *nf* shoulder; [Mex] shoulder of pork

española (a la) *a* (of rice) chicken/seafood/peas/tomato/paprika-garnished

esparcir *vt* [Chile] (of butter) to spread

espárrago *nm* asparagus

espátula *nf* spatula; fish slice

especia *nf* spice

especiado *a* spicy, spiced

especial *a* special; *nm* [SCone] baguette; [Chile] hot-dog

especialidad *nf* speciality

especiar *vt* to spice

especie *nf* species

especiero *nm* spice-rack

espectáculo *nm* floor-show

esperma *nf* [Carib, Colom] candle

espesante *nm* thickener; roux

espesar *vt* (of sauce &c) to thicken

espeso *a* thick

espetón *nm* skewer; spit

espicha *nf* cider party

espiedo *nm* [SCone] spit

espina *nf* (of fish) bone; dorsal spine; thorn; spine

espinaca *nf* spinach; ~**s** spinach

espinazo *nm* spine, backbone

espinilla *nf* shin; shank

espino *nm* hawthorn; ~ **negro** sloe, blackthorn

espinoso *a bony;* thorny; prickly; **grosella** ~**a** gooseberry

espirales *nfpl* pasta variety: twists

espíritu *nm* (of alcohol) spirits

espliego *nm* lavender

espoleta *nf* wishbone

espolón *nm* fetlock

espolvorear *vt* to dust; to

sprinkle (with)

esponjarse *vpr* to become fluffy

esponjoso *a* sponge

espuma *nf* (of beer) froth; head

espumadera *nf* skimmer

espumar *vi* (of wine) to sparkle; (of beer) to froth

espumilla *nf* [LatAm] meringue

espumoso *a* (of beer) frothy; (of wine) sparkling

esquites *nmpl* [CAmer, Mex] popcorn

estación *nf* (of year) season

estacional *a* seasonal

estacionamiento *nm* parking

estadizo *a* off; stale

Estados Unidos *nmpl* United States of America

estancia *nf* farm; cattle farm

estanco *nm* tobacconist's

estearina *nf* [LatAm] candle

estilar *vt* to drain; [Chile] to drip

estirar *vt* to roll out; to stretch out

estofado *a* stewed; *nm* stew, fricassée, hotpot; ~ **irlandés** irish stew

estofar *vt* to stew

estómago *nm* stomach

estoperol *nm* [Andes] frying pan

estopilla *nf* cheesecloth; muslin straining cloth

estragón *nm* tarragon

estrella *nf* star

estrellado *a* (of egg) fried

estrellar *vt* to fry

estropajo *nm* scouring pad

estropajoso *a* (of meat) tough

estropeado *a* (of meat/fruit &c) off

estropearse *vpr* (of meat/fruit &c) to go off

estuche de cubiertos *nm* cutlery canteen

estufa *nf* [Mex] stove

estufilla *nf* small stove

esturión *nm* (of fish) sturgeon

etiqueta *nf* **traje de ~** formal dress; (of bottle) label

etiquetación (etiquetado, etiquetaje *nm*) *nf* labelling

etiquetar *vt* to label

eucalipto *nm* eucalyptus

euro *nm* (of money) euro

eurocheque *nm* eurocheque

Euskadi *nf* Basque country

evacuatorio *nm* public WC

evaporada *a* (of milk) evaporated

evaporar *vt* to evaporate

excusabaraja *nf* hamper

excusado *nm* WC, toilet

exiguo *a* (of quantity) small

expendedor *nm* vending machine

expender *vt* to spend

exprés (expreso) ([Chile] **express)** *nm* espresso coffee; *a* (of coffee) espresso; **olla ~** pressure cooker

exprimelimones *nm* lemon squeezer

exprimidera *nf* squeezer

exprimidor *nm* lemon squeezer

exprimir *vt* (of fruit) to squeeze

exquisito *a* delicious

extracto *nm* extract; essence; ~ **de carne** meat extract; (of tomato) purée

extraordinario *nm* (of menu) special dish; supplementary dish

F

fabada *nf* rich bean/pork stew

fabe *nf* [Asturias] bean

factura *nf* bill; [SCone] cake; bun

fainá *nf* [SCone] savoury pastry

faisán *nm* pheasant

faisanaje *nm* (of game) hanging

fajita *nf* maize pancake

faldas *nfpl* [LatAm] (of meat) flank

falso salmón *nm* sea fish: Brazilian sand-perch

falta (de) *nf* absence (of)

falto (de) *nf* lacking (in)

familia *nf* (of animals) family

faneca (fanega) *nf* Mediterranean flat fish

farináceo *a* starchy; floury

fariña *nf* [SCone, Peru] manioc flour

farra *nf* salmon trout

farsa *nf* stuffing, farce

fauna *nf* fauna

favor (por) *nm* please

faxear *vt* to fax

febrero *nm* February

fecha *nf* date

fécula *nf* starch; ~ **de papa** [LatAm] potato flour

feculento *a* starchy; floury

feo *a* (of lettuce leaves &c) imperfect

festejado (a) *nm/f* birthday/ saint's-day celebrator

festejar *vt* to treat; to fête; to wine and dine; to celebrate

festín *nm* feast, banquet

festinar *vt* to wine and dine

festival *nm* festival

festividad *nf* holiday; feast-day

feta *nm* (of cheese) feta

fiambre *a* (of food) cold; *nm* cold meat; salami sausage; [Mex] pork/avocado/chili

fiambrera *nf* lunch-box

fiambrería *nf* [LatAm] delicatessen

fibra *nf* fibre

ficha *nf* [Mex] bottle-cap

fideo *nm* noodle; ~**s** vermicelli

fideuá *nf* pasta/seafood paella

fierro *nm* knife

fiesta *nf* party; feast-day; holiday

figón *nm* low-price restaurant

figura *nf* shape

filete *nm* steak; (of fish) steak, fillet; escalope; ~ **mignon** (of fillet) mignon; ~ **a la pimienta** pepper steak

filetear *vt* to fillet

film transparente *nm* cling film

filoxera *nf* phylloxera, plant louse

filtrar *vt* to filter

filtro *nm* filter; **cigarrillo con ~** filter-tip cigarette

finca *nf* [Ar] (of wine &c) estate

fino *a* select, fine; (of sherry) dry, fino; *nm* dry sherry

fique *nm* [CAmer] vegetable fibre

flambeado *a* flambé

flambear (flamear) *vt* to flambé

flamenco *a* flemish; *nm* (of music) flamenco

flan *nm* crème caramel; **~ de pescado** (&c) terrine

flanco *nm* flank, side

flanera *nf* jelly mould

flauta *nf* baguette; french bread

flecha de mar *nf* squid

fletán *nm* halibut

flor *nf* flower; **pan de ~** white bread; **~ de** (of ingredient) the finest

flora *nf* flora

floreado *a* (of bread) the finest

florear *vt* to sieve; to sift

florentino *nm* Florentine

fluminense *a* from Rio de Janeiro

flute *nf* (of glass) flute

foca *nf* (of animal) seal

fogata *nf* bonfire

fogón *nm* stove

fogonazo *nm* brandied coffee

foie-gras *nm* foie gras

foil *nm* [Mex] kitchen foil

fonda *nf* small restaurant; [LatAm] low-price restaurant; [SCone] food-stall

fondo *nm* fund; bottom; base; (of dish) [Mex, Ven, Chile] main; (of artichoke) heart; [Chile] low-price restaurant; [Chile] large pot

fonducho (a) *nm/f* low-price restaurant

fondue *nf* fondue

fono *nm* telephone; telephone number

forma *nf* shape; manner

fórmula *nf* recipe

fósforo *nm* match; [Mex] brandied coffee

fotografía *nf* photograph

fragrancia *nf* fragrance

frailecito *nm* [LatAm] plover

frambuesa *nf* raspberry

francés (esa) *a* French; **pan ~** [Ar] baguette; **tortilla francesa** plain/French omelette; **lechuga ~esa** cos lettuce

francesilla *nf* (of bread) roll; French roll

frangipani *nm* frangipane; almond pastry cream

frangollo *nm* [Andes, SCone] corn mash; [SCone] meat/maize stew; [Carib] pulped banana sweet

frankfurt *nm* saveloy; thick sausage; frankfurter

frasco *nm* bottle; jar

frecor *nm* (of drink) coolness

freezer *nm* [LatAm] freezer

fregadero *nm* kitchen sink; scullery

fregador *nm* teacloth; scouring cloth

fregar *vt* to wash-up

fregona *nf* (of person) washer-up

freidera *nf* [Carib] frying pan

freidora *nf* deep-fat frying pan

freiduría de pescado *nf* fried-fish shop

freír *vt* to fry; **~ en mucho aceite** to deep-fry

freírse *vi* to fry

fresa *nf* strawberry

fresco *a* fresh; (of egg) new-laid; (of cheese) unripe; (of drink) cool, cold; *nm* [LatAm] fruit drink

frescura *nf* (of drink) coolness

fresón *nm* strawberry

fresquera *nf* meat safe; cold store

friable *a* friable

fricandó (fricasé) *nm* fricassée; white-sauced stew

fricasé *nm* fricassée; white-sauced stew

friegaplatos *nm/f* (of person) washer-up; (of machine) dish-washer

frigidaire *nm* [LatAm] fridge

frigo *nm* [Spain] fridge; icebox

frigorífico *nm* freezer; fridge

frigorífico-congelador *nm* fridge-freezer

frijol (fríjol) *nm* bean; **~**

colorado kidney bean

frijoles *nmpl* food

frío *a* cold

friorizado *a* deep-frozen

fritada *nf* fry; fry-up; fried dish

fritanga *nf* fry-up, [Andes, CAmer] stew; [CAmer] low-cost restaurant

fritar *vt* [LatAm] to fry

frito *a* fried, **patatas (papas) ~as** [LatAm] chips, French fries; *nm* fried dish; **~s variados** mixed-grill

fritura *nf* fried food; fritter

frízer *nm* [SCone] freezer

fructosa *nf* fructose

fruta *nf* fruit; **~ de la pasión** passion-fruit; **~ del tiempo (~ de (la) estación)** fruit of the season; **~ de sartén** (of fruit) fried, frittered; **~ escarchada (~ confitada)** crystallized fruit

frutal (frutero) *a* fruit

frutera *nf* fruit-bowl

frutería *nf* greengrocer's

frutero *a* fruit; *nm* fruit bowl

frutilla *nf* [Andes, Boliv, SCone] strawberry

fruto *nm* fruit; **~ de pan** breadfruit; **~s secos** dried fruit/nuts

frutosidad *nf* fruity flavour

fuego *nm* fire, heat, flame; (of cigarettes) light; (of cooker) burner; **agua de ~** eau-de-vie, strong spirits

fuente *nf* fountain; spring; serving dish; **~ de hornear (~**

de horno) oven-proof dish; ~ **de soda** soda fountain

fuera *adv* out; outside

fuerte *a* (of drink) strong; *nm* [Chile] strong spirits

fuerza *nf* strength

fugaza *nf* onion pizza

fumadero *nm* smoke-room

fumador (a) *nm/f* smoker; **no ~** no-smoker

fumar *vt* (of tobacco) to smoke

función *nf* function

fundido *a* (of cheese &c) melted

fundir *vt* (of vegetables) to sweat; to fry lightly in oil/butter

G

gabardina *nf* (of prawns) (in) batter

gacel *nm* gazelle

gachas *nfpl* pap; porridge; *nf* [LatAm] earthenware bowl

gajo *nm* (of fruit) segment; slice; (of grapes) small cluster

gallego *a* stew; (of language) galician

galleta *nf* biscuit; [SCone] coarse bread; ~ **agua** water biscuit; ~ **de crema** custard cream; ~ **de campaña** bread variety; ~ **de champaña** [Chile] sponge finger; ~ **salada** cracker; [SCone] maté cup

galletero *nm* biscuit barrel

gallina *nf* chicken; ~ **de Guinea** guinea fowl; ~ **en pepitoria** wine/bread/eggs/nut-sauced chicken; ~ **de bantam** bantam; ~ **de mar** gurnard

gallinazo *nm* [Carib] turkey

gallineta *nf* woodcock; [LatAm] guinea fowl

gallinilla de bantam *nf* bantam

gallipavo *nm* turkey

gallito *nm* cockerel

gallo *nm* (of bird) cock; ~ **lira** black grouse; ~ **silvestre** large grouse, capercaillie; (of fish) dory; ~ **pinto** (CAmer) beans/rice dish; ~ **garapiñada** sugared almond

galón *nm* gallon

galtear *vi* to drip

gamba *nf* prawn; **cóctel de ~s** prawn cocktail; **~s rebozadas** scampi; [Ar] leg

gamo (a) *nm/f* deer (fallow)

gamuza *nf* chamois

ganado *nm* livestock; cattle

gandinga *nf* [Carib] stew

ganso (a) *nm/f* goose; [Ven] (of meat) loin

ganzo *nm* (of beef) stewing cut from prime upper leg

gar(r)apiñar *vt* to freeze; (of cake) to ice; (of fruit) to crystallize

garaje *nm* garage

garapiña *nf* sugar icing; [LatAm] (of drink) iced pineapple

garapiñado *a* (of almond) sugared

garbanzo *nm* chickpea

garbillar *vt* [Ar] to sift; to sieve

garfa *nf* claw

garganta *nf* throat; (of bottle) neck

garnacha *nf* grape variety; sweet wine; [Mex] meat-stuffed tortilla

garrafa *nf* decanter; demijohn

garrafón *nm* demijohn

garrapiñada *nf* sugared almond/peanut

garroba *nf* carob bean

garulla *nf* loose individual grapes

garza *nf* [Chile] lager/beer glass

garzón (ona) *nm/f* [Chile, Urug] waiter (waitress)

gas *nm* gas; **con ~** fizzy; sparkling

gasa *nf* chiffon

gaseado *a* carbonated, fizzy

gaseosa *nf* lemonade; fizzy drink; **~ de jengibre** *nf* ginger ale; ginger beer

gaseoso *a* (of drink) fizzy; sparkling; **~ de jengibre** ginger ale/beer

gastronomía *nf* gastronomy

gastronómico *a* gastronomic

gastrónomo *nm* gastronome; gourmet

gato *nm* [Mex] tip; gratuity

gaucano *nm* [Carib] rum cocktail

gavera *nf* [Venez] (of wine) case; crate

gazapo *nm* young rabbit

gaznate *nm* [Mex] fruit fritter

gazpacho *nm* gaspacho, cold spiced vegetable soup;

[CAmer] (of drink) residue, dregs; (of meal) leftovers

gelatina *nf* gelatin(e); (of meat) brawn

gelatinoso *a* gelatinous

genciana *nf* gentian

género *nm* cloth

generoso *a* (of wine) full-bodied

gerente *nm* manager

germen *nm* shoot; germ

giganta *nf* sunflower

ginebra *nf* gin

ginseng *nm* ginseng

gin-tonic *nm* gin and tonic

girar *vt* to turn

girasol *nm* sunflower

gis *nm* [Mex] pulque

glas *a* (of sugar) icing sugar

glaseado *a* glazed; glacé; with topping

gloriado *nm* hot toddy

glucosa *nf* glucose

glutamato monosódico *nm* monosodium glutamate

gluten *nm* gluten

gobio *nm* freshwater fish; roach, gudgeon

gofio *nm* [LatAm, Canaries] roasted maize

gofre *nm* waffle

gollete *nm* (of bottle) neck

golosina *nf* sweet; titbit

gominola *nf* wine gum

gomita *nf* [Andes] marshmallow

gorda *nf* [Mex] thick tortilla

gordal *nm* olive variety

gordo (a) *nm* suet, fat; *a* oily;

fatty; greasy

gordura *nf* fat; [Carib] cream

gorrino (a) *nm/f* pig; sow

gorrión *nm* sparrow

gorro de cocinero *nm* chef's hat

gota *nf* (of liquid) drop

goteado *a* (of pisco sour) with drops [of whisky]

goulash (goulasch) *nm* goulash; spicy meat/onion stew

gourmet *nm/f* gourmet

gozo *nm* pleasure; enjoyment; delight

¡gracias! *nfpl* thankyou!

grado *nm* (of temperature) degree

graduar *vt* (of temperature) to adjust

graduación *nf* (of alcohol) proof; strength

gragea *nf* small sweet

grajo (a) *nm/f* rook

gramínea *nf* [LatAm] pulse

gramo *nm* gramme

grana *nf* cochineal

granada *nf* (of fruit) pomegranate

granadera *nf* sea fish: grenadier

granadilla *nf* passion fruit

granadina *nf* grenadine

grande *a* large

granel *a* loose; unpackaged; in bulk

granizada *nf* [Andes] iced drink

granizado *nm* crushed-ice(d)

drink

granja *nf* farm; **huevos de ~** free-range eggs; **pollo de ~** free-range chicken

grano *nm* grain, seed; bean; **~ de pimienta** peppercorn

granuja *nf* loose individual grapes

granulado *a* granulated

gránulo *nm* granule

granuloso *a* granular

grapa *nf* [SCone] grappa

grasa *nf* fat; (of fish) oil

grasiento *a* greasy

graso *a* fatty; (of cheese) full-fat

grasoso *a* greasy

gratén (al) *nm* au gratin

gratificación *nf* tip; gratuity

gratín (al) *nm* [Chile] au gratin; with superficial cheese/ breadcrumbs crust

gratinada *nf* au gratin dish

gratinado *a* au gratin; *nm* au gratin dish

gratinador *nm* grill

gratinar *vt* to cook au gratin

gratis *adv* free of charge

gratuitamente *adv* free

gratuito *a* free of charge

gravoso *a* expensive

gravy *nm* gravy

greda *nf* pottery; clay

grei *nm* [Colom] grapefruit

gres *nm* earthenware

grifo *nm* tap; (of beer) draught

grigallo *nm* blackcock

grill *nm* grill; grillroom

grillo *nm* (of plant) shoot

grima *nf* [SCone] (of liquid) drop

grisines *nmpl* [Ar] breadsticks

grosella *nf* redcurrant; ~ **espinosa** gooseberry; ~ **negra** blackcurrant; ~ **colorada** (~ **roja**) redcurrant

grosura *nf* suet; fat

grumo *nm* cluster; (of sauce) lump

grumoso *a* (of sauce &c) lumpy

guacal *nm* large gourd

guacamole *nm* guacamole, avocado/citrus dish

guachalomo *nm* [SCone] sirloin steak

guachinango *nm* [Mex] sea-fish: red snapper

guaje *nm* [Mex] gourd variety

guajolote *nm* turkey

guámparo *nm* [SCone] drinking horn

guanábana *nf* custard apple; soursop

guanaco *nm* guanaco; llama-like Southern Cone animal

guanajo (a) *nm/f* turkey

guarapo *nm* [LatAm] sugar-cane spirits; [Venez] fermented pineapple juice

guarda *nf* (of apple) keeper; long-lasting apple

guardacoches *nm/f* parking attendant

guarnecer *vt* to garnish

guarnición *nf* garnish; accompaniment; trimmings

guaro *nm* [CAmer] spirits; cane-sugar spirits

guarro *nm* pig

guaso (a) (huaso (a)) *nm/f* peasant

guata *nf* ~**s** [Mex] tripe

guatitas *nfpl* [Chile] tripe

guayaba *nf* (LatAm) guava

guayo *nm* [Carib] grater

güegüecho *nm* [CAmer] turkey

güerequeque *nm* [Andes] plover

guerrero *nm* [Carib] rum/vodka cocktail

guía *nf* guidebook

güicoy *nm* [CAmer] courgette

guinda *nf* morello cherry; glacé cherry

guindilla *nf* chili

guindo *nm* morello cherry

Guinea *nf* Guinea; (of bird) guinea fowl

guineo *nm* [LatAm] banana

guirila *nf* [CAmer] maize pancake

guirlache *nm* nougat

guisado *nm* stew; (of meat) stewed/casseroled; ~ **húngaro** goulash

guisador (~a) *nm/f* cook

guisandero (~a) *nm/f* cook

guisante *nm* pea; mange-tout; ~ **majado** split pea

guisantes *nmpl* green peas

guisar *vt* to cook; to stew

guiso *nm* stew; casserole; seasoning; dressing

guisote *nm* hash

güisqui *nm* whisky
güizcal *nm* chayote
gulash *nm* goulash
gulusmear *vt* to nibble; to savour cooking smells
gurrí *nm* [LatAm] wild duck
gusa *nf* hunger; **tener ~** to be hungry
gusgoa *a* [Mex] sweet-toothed
gustar *vt* to please; to taste
gustarse *vi* to like; to enjoy
gusto *nm* taste; flavour; **a ~** (of salt &c) to taste
gustoso *a* tasty

H

haba *nf* broad bean; **~ de soja** soya bean; **~ verde** young broad bean; (of coffee) bean
habano *nm* Havana cigar
haber *vt* to have
habichuela *nf* kidney bean; runner bean
habitación *nf* room
hacer *vt* (of ingredients) to make; to cook; to bake; to brew
hacienda *nf* farm
haleche *nm* anchovy
halibut *nm* halibut
hallaca *nf* banana leaf-wrapped cornmeal/meat/vegetables
hallulla *nf* [Chile] slightly-raised bread
hambre *nf* hunger
hamburguesa *nf* hamburger, burger

hamburguesería *nf* burger bar
harina *nf* flour; **~ de avena** oatmeal; **~ de flor** finely-ground flour; **~ de trigo** wheat flour; **~ con levadura** self-raising flour; **~ de arroz** ground rice; **~ de maíz** cornflour; **~ de patata** potato flour; **~ de soja** soya flour; **~ integral** wholemeal flour; **~ lacteada** malted milk; [Andes] small piece
harinoso *a* floury
harnear *vt* [LatAm] to sift; to sieve
harnero *nm* sieve
hartazgo *nm* glut
hartón *nm* large banana
hayaca *nf* [Carib] cornmeal pasty
hebroso *a* stringy
hecho *a* made, ready, finished; (of cheese, wine) mature; (of fruit) ripe; **muy ~** well-cooked; **poco ~** (of steak) underdone; **muy poco ~** rare
heladera *nf* ice-cream maker; [SCone] fridge
heladería *nf* ice-cream parlour
heladero *a* ice-cream
helado *a* (of drink) ice-cold, iced; **queso ~** ice-cream block; *nm* ice-cream; **~ de agua** water ice
heladora *nf* ice-cream maker; (of fridge) freezer compartment; [SCone] fridge
helar *vt* (of liquid) to freeze; to

ice; to chill

hembra *nf* (of fowl) female; hen

henequén *nm* agave

heñir *vt* to knead

herbario *a* herbal

herbodietético *a* health-food

herméticamente *adv* hermetically

hervido *a* boiled; [LatAm] stew; vegetable/chicken or fish stew; party for such

hervidor *nm* kettle

hervir *vt* to boil; *vi* **empezar a ~ (romper a ~)** to come to the boil; to bubble

hervor *nm* boiling; bringing to the boil

hervoroso *a* boiling

hez *nf* (of wine) lees

hielera *nf* [Chile, Mex] fridge; ice tray

hielo *nm* ice; **con ~** (of drink) with ice, on the rocks; **~ picado** crushed ice

hierba *nf* herb; **a las finas ~s** herbed; **~s finas** mixed herbs, fines herbes; **infusión de ~s** herbal tea; **~ mate** [SCone] maté

hierbabuena *nf* mint

hierro colado *nm* cast iron

hígado *nm* liver; **~ de ganso** goose foie gras

highball *nm* cocktail in a high glass; highball

higiénico *a* hygienic

higo *nm* fig, green fig; **~ chumbo (~ de tuna)** prickly pear; **~ paso (~ seco)** dried fig

hijuelo *nm* shoot

hilera *nf* (of presentation) row; line

hilo *nm* stringy bit; (of liquid) trickle; [Chile] (of potato) alumettes

hinchado *a* (of rice) puffed

hinojo *nm* fennel

hipogloso *nm* halibut

hirviendo *a* boiling

hisopo *nm* (of herb) hyssop; [SCone] teacloth

hogaza *nf* (of bread) large crusty loaf

hoja *nf* leaf; **~ de tocino** flitch; side of bacon; **~ de estaño** kitchen foil; **masa de ~** puff pastry; **~ de laurel** bay leaf; **verduras de ~ verde** (of vegetables) greens

hojalda (hojaldra) *nf* [LatAm] puff pastry

hojaldre *nm* [LatAm] puff pastry

hojuela *nf* pancake; [Carib, Mex] puff pastry

holandesa *a(f)* (of sauce) hollandaise

hollejo *nm* peel; skin

hombrecillo *nm* (of beer) hop

homogénio *a* homogenized

hongo *nm* mushroom; fungus

horchata *nf* tiger nut milk; almond milk

hordiate *nm* barley water

hornada *nf* batch

hornalla *nf* [SCone] oven; ring; burner; hotplate

hornazo *nm* Easter pie; (of cakes, bread) batch

horneado *nm* cooking time

hornear *vt* to bake; to cook in oven

hornero *nm* oven bird

hornillo *nm* cooker

horno *nm* oven; stove; **al ~** baked; **~ de leña** wood-fuelled oven; **~ microondas** microwave

hortaliza *nf* vegetable

hortelano *a* à la jardinière; (of meat) fresh vegetables-casseroled

hospedería *nf* tavern

hostería *nf* inn; tavern; [SCone] hotel

hostigoso *a* (of ingredient) over-sweet

hotel *nm* hotel

hoy *adv* today

huachaiomo *nm* [Chile] (of meat cut) neck

huachinango *nm* sea fish: red snapper

huaiquil (corvinilla) *nf* sea-fish: drum

huaso *nm* [Chile] pork roulade; **~ (a) (guaso (a))** *nm/f* peasant

huemul *nm* [SCone] deer

huepo (navaja de mar) *nm* mollusc: giant Patagonian jack-knife

huerta *nf* vegetable (kitchen) garden

huerto *nm* vegetable (kitchen) garden; market garden; orchard

huesco *nm* bone; **~ de la suerte** wishbone; (of fruit) stone

huesillo *nm* [Andes, SCone] dried peach

hueso *nm* bone

huesoso *a* bony

huésped (a) *nm/f* (of hotel &c) guest; innkeeper

hueva *nf* roe; **~ de lumpo** lumpfish caviar

huevera *nf* egg-cup; [Peru] roe

huevero *a* egg

huevo *nm* egg; **~ a la copa** [Andes] boiled egg; **~ amelcochado** [CAmer] boiled egg; **~ cocido (~ duro)** hard-boiled egg; **~ crudo** raw egg; **~ de corral** free-range egg; **~ en cáscara (~ pasado por agua)** boiled egg; **~ escalfado** poached egg; **~ estrellado (~ frito)** fried egg; **~ de Pascua** Easter egg; **~s al plato** fried eggs/tomato (sauce)/ham/peas; **~s pericos (~s revueltos)** scrambled eggs; **~ tibio** soft-boiled egg

huile *nm* [Mex] roasting grill

huiro *nm* [SCone] seaweed

humeante *a* steaming

húmedo *a* moist

humita *nf* tamale; spiced meat/
maize dish; ground maize;
[SCone] maize leaf-wrapped
ground corn

humo *nm* (of cigarette &c)
smoke

húngaro *a* Hungarian; **guisado**
~ goulash

hure *nm* [Andes] large pot

I

ibérico *a* Iberian

íbice *nm* ibex; goat variety

ibicenco *a* Ibizan

idiazabal *nm* unpasteurized
sheep's milk cheese

iguana *nf* iguana

ijada *nf* **(ijar** *nm*) flank

impedido (a) *nm/f* (of person)
disabled

impotable *a* (of water)
undrinkable; non-drinking

impregnar *vt* to impregnate; to
saturate

improvisado *a* improvised

impuesto *nm* tax; ~ **al valor**
agregado VAT; ~ **sobre**
valor añadido (~ sobre
valor agregado) [LatAm] VAT

inapetente *a* lacking appetite;
not hungry

incapacidad física *nf* physical
handicap

incorporar *vt* to mix in; to fold
in; to add

indio *nm* [CAmer, Mex] maize/
herb-ed meat stew; **pan del** ~

mushroom: indian's bread

inesperado *a* surprise

informal *a* (of dress) casual

infusíon *nf* infusion; ~ **de**
hierbas herbal tea; ~ **de**
manzanilla camomile tea

ingerir *vt* to swallow; to drink

ingesta *nf* ingestion;
consumption

ingestión *nf* ingestion;
consumption

Inglaterra *nf* England

inglés (esa) *a* (of cream)
custard; (of breakfast)
English; cooked

ingrediente *nm* ingredient; ~**s**
[Ar] appetizers; tapas

inmaculado *a* spotless

inmaduro *a* unripe

inmerción *nf* immersion

inocente *nm* [Andes, SCone]
avocado pear

inodoro *nm* bowl; toilet, WC

insípido *a* insipid, tasteless

instantáneo *a* (of coffee)
instant

insulina *nf* insulin

insulsez *nf* tastelessness

insulso *a* tasteless, insipid

integral *a* (of cereal)
wholegrain; (of rice) brown;
(of bread, flour) wholemeal

intemperencia *nf*
intemperence

interdicción *nf* prohibition

interior *nm* inside; ~**es** innards

inválido (a) *nm/f* (of person)
disabled

invernadero *a* (of produce)
  greenhouse; hothouse
invernar *vt* [SCone] to fatten-up
  (in winter)
invierno *nm* winter; [LatAm]
  rainy season
invitado (a) *nm/f* guest
invitar *vt* to invite; to treat
irlandés (esa) *a* (of coffee) irish
italiana (a la) *nf* (of rice) risotto

J

jabalí *nm* wild boar
jabato *nm* young wild boar
jabón *nm* soap
jaiba (jaiva) *nf* [LatAm] crab; ~
  marmola rock crab variety
jáibol *nm* cocktail in a tall glass;
  highball
jalapeño *nm* jalapeño (chili)
  pepper
jalea *nf* jelly; ~ **de guayaba**
  guava jelly; ~ **real** royal jelly
jamón *nm* ham; ~ **de pata**
  negra (~ serrano) Parma
  ham; ~ **dulce (~ (de) York)**
  boiled ham
jamoncito *nm* ham; ~ **crudo**
  Parma ham
japuta *nf* pomfret
jarabe *nm* syrup
jarcia *nf* [CAmer] agave
jardinera *nf* **a la ~** jardinière;
  fresh vegetables-garnished
jarope *nm* syrup
jarra *nf* jug; (of beer) mug; jug
jarrete *nm* hock; [Andes] heel;

knuckle, shin
jarrón *nm* (of flowers) vase
jato *nm* calf
jefe (a) *nm/f* chef
jengibre *nm* ginger
jerez *nm* sherry
jerguilla *nf* sea-fish: marble fish
jibia (calamar rojo) *nf*
  cuttlefish; jumbo squid
jícama *nf* [CAmer] tuber; yam
  bean
jícara *nf* chocolate cup; [CAmer,
  Mex] gourd; *nm* bowl
jifia *nf* swordfish
jigote *nm* meat stew
jijona *nm* nougat
jimba *nf* [Mex] bamboo
jira campestre *nf* picnic
jitomate *nm* [Mex] tomato
jobo *nm* [CAmer] (of drink)
  spirits
jocoque (jocoqui) *nm* [Mex]
  sour milk; sour cream
jojoba *nf* jojoba
jojoto *a* [Carib] (of fruit)
  bruised; unripe; [LatAm] maize
jolote *nm* [CAmer, Mex] turkey
jora *nf* [LatAm] maize
judía *nf* bean; ~ **blanca** haricot;
  ~ **colorada (~ escarlata)**
  runner; ~ **de la peladilla (~**
  de Lima) Lima bean; ~**s**
  verdes french beans
juego *nm* set; service; ~ **de**
  café coffee service; ~ **de**
  mesa dinner service; ~ **de té**
  tea set; ~**s verdes** french
  beans

jueves *nm/adv* Thursday

jugo *nm* juice; (of lemon &c) lemon juice; (of meat &c) gravy

jugosidad *nf* juiciness; succulence

jugoso *a* juicy; succulent; moist

juguera *nf* [SCone] liquidizer, blender

juilipío *nm* [Andes] sparrow

julepe *nm* (drink) julep

juliana *nf* julienne, thinly-sliced vegetable; **sopa ~** vegetable consommé

julio *nm* July

jumilla *nm* spanish wine variety

junio *nm* June

junta *nf* re-union; meeting

junto *a* together

jupa *nf* [CAmer] gourd; calabash

jurel *nm* sea fish: horse mackerel

justificante *nm* receipt

jute *nm* [CAmer] snail

K

kanikama *nf* seafood stick

kebab *nm* kebab

kéfir *nm* [Andes] yoghurt

ketchup *nm* ketchup

kiko *nm* toasted maize

kilo *nm* kilo

kilocaloría *nf* calorie

kilogramo *nm* kilogramme

kilómetro *nm* kilometre

kimbombó *nm* okra, (of vegetable) tropical plant

kiwi *nm* kiwi fruit

krill antartico *nm* krill

kuchen *nm* [Chile] German cake

L

labio *nm* rim; edge; lip

lacón *nm* shoulder of pork

lácteo *a* milk

láctico *a* lactic

lacto-ovo-vegetariano (a) *a* milk-egg-vegetarian

lactosa *nf* lactose

lactosuero *nm* whey

lado *nm* side

lagar *nm* winery

lago *nm* lake

lagrimilla *nf* [SCone] unfermented grape juice

lámina *nf* (of cheese &c) slice; sliver

lamparín *nm* [SCone] candle

lampazo *nm* burdock

lamprea *nf* (of fish) lamprey; eel-like fish

langosta *nf* seafish: lobster; (of river) crayfish

langostino (langostín) *nm* prawn; king prawn; Dublin Bay prawn; tiger prawn

lapa *nf* mollusc: limpet; [SCone] gourd bowl

lardar *vt* to lard, to baste

lardo *nm* lard

largo *a* long

lasaña (lasagna) *nf* lasagna, lasagne

lasca *nf* slice

lata *nf* tin, can; [Andes] food
laurel *nm* laurel; [Chile] bay;
  hoja de ~ bay leaf
lavabo *nm* toilet, WC
lavador *nm* [SCone] toilet, WC
lavafrutas *nm* finger bowl
lavagallos *nm* [Andes, Carib]
  eau-de-vie; strong fruit brandy
lavanda *nf* lavender
lavaplatos *nm/f* (of person)
  washer-up; (of machine) dish-
  washer
lavar *vt* to wash
lavavajillas *nm* (of machine)
  dishwasher; washing-up liquid
lebrato *nm* leveret, young hare
lebrillo *nm* earthenware bowl
lecha *nf* soft roe
lechal *a* (of young animal)
  suck(l)ing; milky
lechazo *nm* young lamb
leche *nm* milk; **~ completa (~
  entera)** full-cream milk; **~ del
  día** fresh milk; **~ descremada**
  skimmed milk; **~ en polvo**
  powdered milk; **~ evaporada**
  evaporated milk; **~ frita**
  thickened-milk pudding; **~
  pasteurizada** pasteurised
  milk; **~ condensada**
  condensed milk; **café con ~**
  white coffee; **chocolate con
  ~** milk chocolate; **~ frita** (of
  dessert) milk/flour/egg-fried; **~
  merengada** cinnamon
  milkshake; **~ de coco** coconut
  milk; **~ de larga duración**
  long-life milk

lechecillas *nfpl* sweetbreads
lechera *nf* [LatAm] cow
lecherita *nf* milk-jug
lechero *nm* milk
lechón (ona) *nm/f* suck(l)ing
  pig
lechoncillo *nm* suck(l)ing pig
lechosa *nf* [CAmer, Venez]
  papaya
lechosidad *nf* milkiness
lechoso *a* milky
lechucero *nm* (of night-time)
  taxi
lechuga *nf* lettuce; **~ cos (~
  francesa) (~ orejona** [Mex])
  (~ costina [Chile]) cos lettuce
lechuguino *nm* young lettuce
legarto *nm* lizard
legartija *nf* small lizard
legumbre *nf* vegetable; pulses
lengua *nf* tongue
lenguado *nm* sole; dab;
  flounder
lenteja *nf* lentil
lentejas *nfpl* lentil soup
lento *a* (of heat/oven) low;
  slow
leña *nf* firewood; **carbon de ~**
  charcoal
leonesa *nf* [Chile] wedge
levadura *nf* yeast; **~ en polvo**
  baking powder
levantamuertos *nm* [Andes]
  vegetable soup
levantar los manteles *vt* to
  clear the table
libar *vt* to taste; to sip
libre *nm* [Mex] taxi

libreta *nf* (of bread) loaf

librillo (en) *nm* [Chile] (of shellfish) in earthenware pot

libro *nm* ~ **de honor** (~ **de visitas**) visitors' book; ~ **de reclamaciones** complaints book; ~ **de cocina** cookbook

lichi *nm* lychee

líchigo *nm* [Andes] food

licor *nm* liqueur; **~es** spirits

licorera *nf* decanter

licoroso *a* (of wine &c) strong; highly-alcoholic

licuado de frutas *nm* [LatAm] milk-shake

licuadora *nf* blender; liquidizer

licuar *vt* to blend; to liquidize

liebre *nf* hare

liga *nf* mistletoe

ligar *vt* (of sauce) to thicken; (of drinks) to mix

ligeramente *adv* lightly; slightly

ligero *a* light

light *a* (of meal) low-calorie; (of tobacco) low-tar

lija *nf* dogfish

Lima *nf* (of bean) Lima

lima *nf* lime

limeta *nf* bottle

limón *nm* lemon; [Carib] lime; **crema de ~** lemon curd

limonada *nf* lemonade; lemon squash; **~ natural** lemon pressé

limpiadientes *nm* toothpick

limpiahornos *nm* oven-cleaner

limpiamanos *nm* [CAmer] hand-towel

limpiar *vt* (of poultry/game) to clean; (of fish) to clean, to gut

limpión *nm* [CAmer, Andes] dishcloth

liofilizado *a* freeze-dried

líquida *nf* liquid

líquido *a* liquid, fluid; (of cream) single cream; *nm* liquid, fluid

lisa *nf* [Carib, LAm] beer; [Andes] sea fish: mullet; [Mex] sea fish: cod; river fish: loach; [Ar] sea/freshwater fish: liza

liso *nm* [SCone] tall beer glass; (of ribs of beef &c) lower

lista *nf* menu; ~ **de vinos** wine list; ~ **de espera** waiting list; ~ **de compras** shopping list

listo *a* ready

litro *nm* litre

livianos *nmpl* (of offal) lights

llama *nf* flame

llamar *vt* to telephone; to call

llantén *nm* plantain

llapingacho *nm* [Andes] cheese omelette

llave *nf* (of door) key

llegar *vi* to arrive; to put (in); to place (in)

llenador *a* (of meal) filling

llenar *vt* to fill

lleno *a* (of glass &c) full

llevar *vt* (of oven &c) to place (in); to remove to; (of food) **para ~** take-away

lobo *nm* seal

loca *nm* [Chile] abalone, mollusc variety

locería *nf* chinaware

locha nf freshwater fish: loach; carp variety

loco nm mollusc: false abalone

locrear vi to eat, to have a meal

locro nm [LatAm] meat/veg stew; meat/maize stew

locumba nf [Peru] grape eau-de-vie

locutorio nm telephone booth

lombarda nf (of vegetables) red cabbage

lomo nm loin, back; ~s ribs; ~ **embuchado** [Spain] cured pork loin; [LatAm] fillet of steak

loncha (lonja) nf slice; (of bacon) rasher

lonchar vi to have lunch; vt [LatAm] to lunch somebody

lonche nm [LatAm] lunch; tea

lonchera nf [Andes] lunch box

lonchería nf [LatAm] snack bar

loncho nm [Andes] slice, piece

longaniza nf long pork sausage

lonja (loncha) nf slice; (of bacon) rasher; market

loro nm sea-fish: parrotfish

lota nf freshwater fish: burbot

loza nf crockery; ~ **fina** china

lubina nf sea bass

lucerna nf chandelier

luche nm [SCone] seaweed

lucio nm freshwater fish: pike

lúcuma nf aubergine, eggplant; [Andes] eggfruit

lugánica nf Italian sausage

lugareño a local; regional

lugo nm [Andes] ram

lumbre nf stove

lumpo nm lumpfish

luna de miel nf honeymoon

lunch nm lunch; cold buffet

lunes nm/adv Monday

lúpulo nm hops

luz del sol nf sunshine

M

maca nf (of fruit) bruise; defect

macarrón nm macaroon

macarrones nmpl macaroni; ~ **gratinados (~ con queso)** macaroni cheese

macedonia de frutas nf fruit salad, fruit cocktail; ~ **de verduras** mixed vegetables; macedoine

maceración nf (of fruit) soaking; (of meat) marinade

macerar vt (of fruit) to soak; (of meat) to marinate

maceta nf [SCone] bouquet

macha nf razor clam

machacar vt to pound; to crush

machito nm [Mex] fried offal

macho nm (of animal) male

machucar vt (of fruit) to bruise; to crush

machuelo (tritre) nm sea-fish: Pacific menhaden

macis nf (of spice) mace

madalena nf Genoese cake

madera nm (of fortified wine) Madeira

madre nf (of wine) sediment, lees

madreperla de río nf

freshwater mussel

madrileña (a la) *a* tomato/onion/pepper/ham-garnished

maduración *nf* maturation

madurar *vi* (of fruit) to ripen

maduro *a* (of fruit) ripe; *nm* [LatAm] plantain

magdalena *nf* Genoese cake

magra *nf* (of meat) lean; slice; (of bacon) rasher

magras *nfpl* (of dish) fried-egg/ham/cheese/tomato

magro *a* (of meat) lean

maguey *nm* maguey; agave variety

magullar *vt* (of fruit) to bruise

mahonesa *nf* mayonnaise

maicena *nf* cornflour

maicero *a* maize

maître *nm* head waiter

maíz *nm* maize, sweetcorn, **~ en la mazorca** corn on the cob; **~ pira** popcorn

maja (majador *nm)* *nf* pestle

majoleta *nf* hawthorn berry; young vine

majuelo (a) *nm/f* hawthorn berry

mal *a* bad; off

Málaga *nf* sweet fortified wine

malanga *nf* sweet potato variety

malaya *nf* [Chile] steak

malbec *nm* [esp Ar] wine variety

mallorquín (ina) *a* Majorcan

malo *a* bad; off

malta *nf* malt; [Chile] dark beer;

whisky de ~ malt whisky

malteada *nf* [LatAm] malted milk shake

malteado *a* malted; *nm* malting

maltear *vt* to malt

malton *nm* [Chile] Chilean mussel

malva *nf* mallow

malvasía *nf* malmsey; sweet white wine variety

malvavisco *nm* marshmallow

mamaón *nm* [Mex] tipsy cake, wined custard cake

mamón *nm* [CAmer] sponge cake; [SCone] papaya; (of plant) shoot

mana (maná *nm)* *nf* manna

manantial *nm* (of water) spring water; running water

mancha (la) *nm* spanish wine variety

manchar *vt* (with wine &c) to stain

manchego (queso) *a* ewe's milk cheese

mandar *vt* (of waiter) to order

mandarina *nf* mandarin; tangerine

mandioca *nf* (of flour) manioc; cassava; tapioca

mandolina *nf* (of fruit &c) mandolin(e), multi-bladed knife

manduvá *nf* freshwater fish: manduba

manera *nf* way; method; style

manga *nf* strainer; **~ pastelera** piping bag; mango variety

mango *nm* mango

manguruyú *nm* freshwater fish: manguruyú

maní *nm* peanut; monkeynut; groundnut

manija *nf* [SCone] mug

manir *vt* (of meat) to hang

manita *nf* (of pig) trotter

manjar *nm* delicacy [SCone] hot condensed milk; ~ **blanco** blanc-mange; [Andes] caramel spread; ~ **dulce** [Andes] fudge

mano *nf* hand; trotter; foot; pestle

manojo *nm* bunch

manteca *nf* butter; ~ **de cerdo** lard; ~ **de cacahete** peanut butter; ~ **de cacao** cocoa butter; ~ **de vaca** butter; ~ **vegetal** vegetable fat

mantecada *nf* iced bun; small cake

mantecado *nm* almond/lard Christmas sweet; dairy ice-cream; fairy cake

mantecoso *a* creamy, buttery; **queso ~** soft cheese

mantel *nm* tablecloth; ~ **individual** place mat

mantelería *nf* table linen

mantequera *nf* [RPlate] butter dish

mantequilla *nf* butter; ~ **de cacahuete** peanut butter

mantequillera *nf* butter dish

manuelita *nf* [Carib] rolled pancake

manzana *nf* apple; ~ **ácida** cooking apple; ~ **de mesa** eating apple; ~ **silvestre** crabapple

manzanilla *nf* camomile; camomile tea; camomile liqueur; small olive; dry sherry

mañana *adv* tomorrow

mañoco *nm* [Venez] cassava; manioc flour

máquina picadora *nf* mincer

mar *nm* sea; ~ **y tierra** surf and turf

maracuyá *nm* passion fruit

marañón *nm* cashew nut

maravilloso *a* marvellous

marca *nf* brand; label

margarina *nf* margarine

margarita *nf* margarita; tequila/lime cocktail; mollusc: winkle

marasquino (marrasquino) *nm* maraschino; bitter cherries liqueur

maridaje *nm* (of foods/ingredients &c) marriage; combination; accompaniment

marinado *a* marinated; **~a** [LAmer] salt meat

marinar *vt* to marinate, to marinade

marinero *a* (of fish) sea; marine

marino *a* sea

mariscada *nf* seafood platter

mariscal *nm* [Chile] seafood compote

marisco *nm* seafood, shellfish; mollusc: mussels; **cóctel de ~s** seafood cocktail

marisquería nf seafood restaurant

marisquero a seafood; shellfish

marmita nf marmite; earthenware cooking-pot

marmitón nm kitchen boy

mármol nm kitchen slab

marquezote nm [CAmer] bread

marrajo (tiburón) nm shark

marrano nm/f pig (sow); [Colom] pork

marraqueta nf bread roll

marrasquino (marasquino) nm maraschino; (of bitter cherries) liqueur

marrón a [Carib] white coffee; ~ **glacé** marron glacé

marroncito nm [Carib] white coffee

marsopa nf porpoise

martes nm/adv Tuesday; **martes de carnaval** n Shrove Tuesday; Mardi Gras

marucha nf [Andes] rump steak

marzo nm March

más adv more

masa nf dough; pastry; batter; [SCone] bun; [Andes, SCone] puff pastry; ~ **quebrada** shortcrust pastry; [Mex] ~ **harina** cornflour; ~ **de hojaldre** puff pastry

masato nm [Andes, CAmer] fermented maize/rice/banana &c drink; [Andes] coconut sweet; [Andes] banana custard

mascar vt to chew

masita nf [LatAm] pastry; cake

masitero nm [Andes, Carib, SCone] pastry-cook; confectioner

mastuerzo nm cress; ~ **de agua** watercress

mata nf sprig; bunch; (of celery) head; shrub; plant; tree

matacán nm young deer; [CAmer] calf

matadero nm abattoir

matafuego nm fire-extinguisher

matalahúga (matalahúva) nf aniseed

matambre nm [SCone] stuffed meat roulade; (of meat) flank; skirt

matanza nf abattoir; [Andes] butcher's shop

matar vt (of cattle &c) to slaughter

mate nm [LatAm] maté; maté cup; gourd cup (for maté)

matear vi [LatAm] to drink maté

mayo nm May

mayonesa nf mayonnaise

mayordomo nm butler

mazacote nm lumpy mess

mazamorra nf [LatAm] maize porridge

mazapán nm marzipan

mazo nm pestle; (of meat) tenderizer

mazorca nf (of maize) cob

meaja nf crumb

mecato nm [Andes]

pâtisseries; [Colom] pack-
lunch

mechado *a* (of meat) larded

mechar *vt* (of bacon) to lard; to
stuff

mechero *nm* cigarette lighter

mecho *nm* [Andes, CAmer]
candle; candlestick

medallón *nm* round slice,
medallion; ~ **de pescado** fish
cake

media *nf* (of beer) quarter litre
bottle

medialuna *nf* croissant

mediano *a* medium-sized

medianoche *nf* late meal eaten;
sandwich roll

medida *nf* measure

medio *a* half; average; **~a
pensión**; dinner, bed &
breakfast, half-board

mediodía *nm* lunch-time

medir *vt* to measure

mediterráneo *a* Mediterranean

médula ósea *nf* bone marrow

mejido *a* (of egg) beaten

mejillón *nm* mussel; **~es a la
marinera** moules marinières

mejillonero *a* mussel

mejorana *nf* (of herb) marjoram

mejunje *nm* concoction; brew

melado *nm* syrup, treacle;
[LatAm] cane syrup

meladura *nf* [Carib, Mex] cane
syrup

melaza *nf* molasses, treacle

melcocha *nf* treacle; molasses
toffee

melcochado *a* (of fruit)
crystallized

melcocharse *vi* (of boiling) to
thicken

melindre *nm* iced bun; cake;
honey fritter

melocotón *nm* peach; star-fruit

melón *nm* melon

meloso *a* sweet

membrillo *nm* quince; **carne
de ~** quince jelly

memela *nf* [CAmer, Mex] maize
tortilla; bean-ed fried tortilla

mendrugo *nm* (of bread)
crust; stale bread

menear *vt* (of liquid) to stir

menestra *nf* (of vegetable)
stew; (of ingredients) mixed
vegetables

menestrón *nm* [Andes]
minestrone soup

menos *adv* less

mensáfono *nm* pager; bleeper

mensaje *nm* message

menta *nf* mint; ~ **romana (~
verde)** spearmint

méntrida *nm* spanish wine
variety

menú *nm* menu; ~ **de la casa**
main/standard menu; ~ **del
día** [Spain] set menu; meal

menudencias *nfpl* (of pork)
offal; (of fowl) giblets

menudillos *nmpl* giblets

menudo *a* finely chopped

menudos *nmpl* offal; (of fowl)
giblets; [Mex] tripe stew

meollo *nm* (of bread) soft part;

crumb

mercado *nm* market; **~ de abastos** food market

mercancía en depósito *nf* bonded goods

mercancías perecederas *nfpl* perishable goods

Mercosur *nm* Argentine/Brazil/ Paraguay/Uruguay economic community

merendar *vi* to have tea; to picnic

merendero *nm* alfresco café; picnic area/place

merendola *nf* tea party, picnic

merengada *nf* [Venez] milkshake

merengue *nm* meringue; **~ blando** (of sweets) marshmallow

merienda *nf* (of meal) tea; packed meal, picnic; [Andes] supper; **~~-cena** high tea

merino *a* (of lamb) merino

merlan *nm* sea fish: whiting

merlango *nm* sea fish: haddock

merlo *nm* sea fish: wrasse

merluza *nf* sea fish: hake; [Chile] **~ de cola** Patagonia whiphake; **~ de tres aletas** southern blue whiting; **~ del sur** Patagonia hake

mermar *vt* to reduce

mermelada *nf* jam, **~ de naranja** marmalade

mero *nm* sea fish: grouper; rock cod; [Ar] Argentine sea bass

mes *nm* month

mesa *nf* table; **¡a la ~!** lunch (&c) is ready!

mescal *nm* mescal, cactus spirit

mesero (a) *nm/f* [Mex] waiter (waitress)

mesón *nm* old style tavern; [SCone] large table

mesonero (a) *nm/f* [Carib] waiter/waitress

mestizo (a) *nm/f* crossbreed

método *nm* method

mez(z)anine *nm* mezzanine

mezcla *nf* mixture; blend; **~ para rebozar** batter

mezclador *nm* **vaso ~** mixing bowl

mezclar *vt* to mix; to blend; to combine

miaja *nf* crumb

miche *nm* [Carib] spirits

microondas *nm* (of oven) microwave

miel *nf* honey; **~ de palma/ maíz/caña** palm/corn/sugar- cane syrup

mielero *nm* honey pot

mielga *nf* alfalfa

miércoles *nm/adv* Wednesday

mies *nf* ripe grain

miga *nf* soft part of bread; **~s** fried breadcrumbs

migajas *nfpl* crumbs

mijo *nm* millet

milanesa *nf* [esp LatAm] escalope; wiener schnitzel

milhojas *nm/f* millefeuille; meringue-filled millefeuille

miligramo *nm* milligramme

mililitro *nm* millilitre

millo (millón) *nm* [CAmer] millet

miltomate *nm* [CAmer, Mex] (of tomato) small green/white variety

mimosa *nf* mimosa

mineral *a* mineral

minestrone (minestrón [LatAm] *nm/f*) *nf* minestrone

minihorno *nm* small stove

mínimo *nm* minimum

minusválido *a* disabled

minuta *nf* menu; [Carib, SCone] **a la ~** breadcrumbed; [CAmer] ice drink; [RPlate] quick meal

minuto *nm* (of time) minute

mirabelle *nm* mirabelle

mirasol *nm* sunflower

mirlo *nm* blackbird

mirtilo *nm* bilberry; whortleberry

mirto *nm* myrtle

misera *nf* lobster

mistela *nf* [Chile] hot punch

mitad *nf* half

mitigar *vt* (of thirst) to quench

mítulo *nm* mussel

mixto *a* mixed; *nm* toasted two-fillings sandwich; (of cigarette) match

moca (moka) *nm* mocha; *nf* [Mex] coffee cake/biscuit

modo *nm* method; manner; way

modorro *a* (of fruit) soft, pulpy

mogolla *nf* [Colom] bread-roll

mojama *nf* salted tuna

mojar *vt* to wet; to dampen; to dunk

mojarra *nf* [LatAm] short broad knife; sea fish: bream variety

mojicón *nm* sponge finger; bun

mojito *nm* [Cuba] rum-based drink

mojo *nm* garlic sauce

molde *nm* mould; **pan de ~** tin loaf

moldecito *nm* small mould

mole *nm* [Mex] chile sauce; [Mex] (of meat) chile sauced; [Mex] **~ de olla** meat stew

moler *vt* (of coffee) to grind; to pound; to crush

molido *a* (of coffee/spices &c) ground; (of meat) minced; (of ice) crushed

molinillo *nm* (of coffee &c) mill; (of meat) mincer; [Mex] whisk

molla *nf* (of meat) lean; (of fruit) flesh; (of bread) soft centre; crumb

mollar *a* (of fruit) soft; easy-to-peel; (of nut) easily shelled; (of meat) boned

molledo *nm* (of bread) doughy part

molleja *nf* (of fowl) gizzard; stomach; **~s** (of cow/lamb) sweetbreads

mollete *nm* muffin

molote *nm* [Mex] maize pancake

molusco *nm* mollusc

momio *a* (of meat) lean

mona de pascua *nf* Easter Cake

monda *nf* (of orange/potato &c) peel

mondadientes *nm* toothpick; cocktail stick

mondar *vt* (of fruit/potato &c) to peel; (of nuts/peas &c) to shell

mondéjar nm spanish wine variety

mondongo *nm* tripe

moneda *nf* coin; (of country) currency

mono *nm* monkey; **cola de ~** [Chile] milk/coffee/vanilla rum punch

montadito *nm* [Spain] small sandwich

montado *a* (of cream) whipped; (of egg white) whisked; *nm* [Spain] small sandwich; **~ de lomo** hot pork sandwich

montaña *nf* mountain

montaplatos *nm* dumb-waiter

montar *vt* (of cream) to whip; (of egg white) to whisk, to beat

montaraz *a* (of animal) wild

monte *nm* mountain; hill; woodland; countryside

monterrei *nm* spanish wine variety

montés *a* wild

montilla *nm* pale dry sherry

montoncito *nm* small heap

montuno *a* mountain; forest

mora *nf* blackberry; mulberry; black pudding

morapio *nm* red plonk

morcilla *nf* black pudding; [Mex] tripe

morcillo *nm* (of beef) shank

morcón *nm* large blood sausage

morena *nf* sea fish: moray eel

moreno *a* (of bread &c) brown

morera *nf* white mulberry

morfar *vi* [RPlate] to eat

moro/a *nm* [Carib] beans/rice dish

morocho *nm* maize

moronga *nf* [CAmer, Mex] black pudding; blood sausage

morralla *nf* small fish; whitebait

morrocoy (morrocoyo) *nm* [CAmer] turtle

morrón *nm* sweet red pepper

mortadela *nf* mortadella; cooked spicy myrtleberry sausage

moruno *a* **pincho ~** kebab

moscada *a* (of spice/nut) nutmeg

moscatel *nm/a* muscatel

moscón *nm* maple

mostacero (a) *nm/f* mustard pot

mostachón *nm* macaroon

mostaza *nf* mustard; **~ de Dijon** french mustard; **~ inglesa** english mustard

mosto *nm* grape juice; (of wine) must

mote *nm* [Andes] boiled wheat; boiled maize; **~ con huesillos**

[Chile] maize/peach drink; sea fish: whiting variety

mousse *nf* mousse

mover *vt* to stir

mozo (a) *nm/f* waiter; barmaid

mozzarella *nf* mozzarella; cow's milk cheese

múcura *nf* [Andes, Carib] earthenware jug

mueble-bar *nm* drinks cabinet

muégano *nm* [Mex] caramel sweet

muérdago *nm* mistletoe

muesli *nm* muesli

mugrón *nm* shoot; sprout

mújol *nm* sea fish: grey mullet

mulata (vieja) *nf* sea fish: wrasse

mullo *nm* sea fish: red mullet

multicolor *a* multi-coloured

musaca *nf* moussaka, cheesed aubergined lamb/beef

muselina *nf* muslin

muslo *nm* drumstick; thigh

N (for Ñ see end of N)

naba *nf* swede

nabo *nm* turnip; root vegetable; ~ **sueco** swede

nacatamal *nm* [CAmer, Mex] banana leaf-wrapped maize/meat/rice

nacho *nm* nacho; savoury crisp

nacional *a* indigenous

naco *nm* ; mashed potatoes; [Andes, SCone] salted maize kernels

nada *pron* nothing; [RPlate] (of liquid/solid) drop; pinch

nalga *nf* [SCone] rumpsteak

nalgada *nf* ham

nanue *nm* sea fish: nibbler; sea chub

napolitano *a* Neapolitan

naranja *nf* orange; ~ **amarga (~ cajel) (~ zajarí)** Seville orange; ~ **sanguina** blood orange; [Carib] bitter orange

naranjada *nf* orangeade; orange squash

nariz *nf* (of wine) nose

nasa *nf* bread-bin

nata *nf* [Spain] cream; ~ **líquida** cream; ~ **batida (~ montada)** whipping cream; ~ **de huevo** egg custard

natillas *nfpl* [Spain] custard

natural *a* without additives, organic, natural; (of fruit) fresh; (of wine) at room temperature; unchilled

navaja de mar (huepo) *nf* mollusc: giant Patagonian knifejack; sea asparagus

navajuela *nf* mollusc: Chilean knifejack

navideño *a* christmas

nécora *nf* small crab

néctar *nm* nectar

nectarín *nm* nectarine

nectarina *nf* nectarine

negrito *nm* [Carib] black coffee

negro *a* black; **grosella ~a** blackcurrant

negro *nm* [Carib] black coffee

nervadura *nf* (of peppers &c) internal vein

nervio *nm* sinew; gristle

neto *a* (of price) net

nevera *nf* fridge

nevera-congelador *nf* fridge-freezer

nido *nm* nest

nieve *nf* snow; (of egg-white) **a punto de ~** beaten stiff; [LatAm] ice lolly; sorbet, water-ice

niño (a) *a* (of fruit) unripe, green; young

níspero (níspola) *nm* (of fruit) medlar

nivel *nm* level

nixtamal *nm* cooked sweetcorn

nochote *nm* [Mex] cactus beer

nogada *nf* (for fish) spicy nutty sauce

nogado *nm* (of dish) walnutted

nogal *nm* walnut tree

nopal *nm* prickly pear

nota *nf* (of bill) receipt

noviembre *nm* November

nube *nf* candyfloss

núcleo *nm* kernel; stone

nudillo *nm* knuckle

nueces *see* nuez

nuégado *nm* nougat

nueve *a* nine; *nm* nine; ninth

nuevo *a* new

nuez *(pl* **nueces)** *nf* nut; walnut; [Mex] pecan nut; **~ de Brasil** (**~ de Pará**) Brazil nut; **~ de Castilla** ([Mex] **~ nogal**) walnut; **~ moscada** nutmeg

número *nm* number; **~ de teléfono** telephone number; **~ de matrícula** vehicle registration number

nupcias *nfpl* wedding

nutrición *nf* nutrition

nutrido *a* nourished

nutrimento *nm* nourishment

nutrir *vt* to nourish; to feed

nutritivo *a* nourishing; nutritious

Ñ

ñaco *nm* [Mex] popcorn

ñame *nm* yam

ñandú *nm* rhea

ñoqui *nm* **~s** gnocchi; small dumplings

ñora *nf* variety of hot pepper

O

oblea *nf* thin slice

obsequio de *nm* with the compliments of

oca *nf* goose; [Andes] (of root vegetable) oca

ocho *a* eight

octubre *nm* October

ocupado *a* (of toilet &c) occupied

oferta *nf* special offer

oficio *nm* scullery

ojén *nm* anisette, aniseed liqueur

ojo *nm* eye

OLAVU (Organización Latinoamericana del Vino y

de la Uva) *nf* Latin-American Organization for Wine and Grape

oleícola *a* (of horticulture) oil

olfatear *vt* to smell

oliscar *vt* to sniff

oliva *nf* olive; **~ virgen** virgin olive oil; *a* olive

olivarero *a* olive

olivero *a* olive

olla *nf* pot, pan; stew; **~ a (~ de) presión (~ exprés)** pressure cooker; **~ podrida** stew; **~ común (~ popular)** [SCone] soup kitchen

olor *nm* smell; **~es** [SCone, Mex] spices; **clavo de ~** clove

olorcillo *nm* delicate aroma

oloroso *nm* (of sherry) oloroso, medium sweet sherry

olote *nm* corncob

onces *nfpl* elevenses; [Andes] tea

oporto *nm* port

opuncia *nf* [Mex] prickly pear

orden *nm* [Mex] dish

oreado *a* (of meat) dried

orear *vt* (of meat) to dry

orégano *nm* oregano

oreja *nf* ear; handle; **~ marina** abalone; ormer ; sea-ear; large shelled mollusc

orejón *nm* dried peach/apricot; [Chile] **~ de membrillo** quince; *a* **lechuga ~a** cos lettuce

orejudo *nm* [LatAm] dried peach/apricot

orgánico *a* organic

origen *nm* origin

orilla *nf* rim; edge; (of bread) crust

orinacamas *nm* dandelion

Orinoco *nm* Orinoco River

oriundo *a* (of plants &c) indigenous

orozuz *nm* liquorice

ortiga *nf* nettle

oruga *nf* (of salad) rocket

orujo *nm* grape eau-de-vie

orza *nf* earthenware jug

oscurecer *vt* to darken; to discolour

óseo *a* bony

osobuco *nm* veal stew; osso buco

ostión *nm* large oyster; [SCone] Patagonian scallop

ostionería *nf* [LatAm] seafood restaurant; oyster bar

ostra *nf* oyster

ostrería *nf* oyster bar

otoñal *a* autumnal; autumn

otoño *nm* autumn

ovas *nfpl* (of fish) roe

oveja *nf* ewe, female sheep

ovejo (ovejón) *nm* ram

ovejuno *a* sheep

overbooking *nm* overbooking

overear *vt* [SCone] to brown

ovino *nm* mutton; lamb

ovolactovegetariano (a) *nm/f* lacto-ovo-vegetarian; *a* lacto-ovo-vegetarian

ovovegetariano (a) *nm/f* ovo-vegetarian; *a* ovo-vegetarian

oxiacanta *nf* hawthorn

P

pacú *nm* freshwater fish: giant pacu

pábulo *nm* food

pacana *nf* pecan

pachamanca *nf* [Peru] barbecue

pacharán *nm* sloe gin

pachucho *a* over-ripe

Pacífico *a* Pacific Ocean

paella *nf* paella; paella dish

paellera *nf* (of crockery) paella dish

paellero (a) *nm/f* paella cook

paellero *a* paella

pagar *vt* to pay

pago *nm* payment; **~ a la orden (~ domiciliado)** direct debit; **~ al contado** cash payment; **~ con tarjeta de crédito** by credit card

pagua *nf* [Mex] avocado pear

paguacha *nf* melon

paguala *nf* [Carib] swordfish

pai *nm* [LatAm] pie; **~ de queso** cheesecake

paiche *nm* [Andes] dried salted fish

paila *nf [esp* Chile] frying pan, [SCone] fry-up

pailón *nm* [Andes, Carib] pot, pan

país *nm* country; region; **vino del ~** wine from locality

paja *nf* drinking straw

pájara *nf* hen bird

pájaro *nf* bird

pajel *nm* sea-bream

pajilla *nf* [LatAm] maize cigarette

pajita (pajilla) *nf* drinking straw

pala *nf* slice

paladar *nm* (of taste) palate; offal

paladear *vt* to savour, to taste

paladeo *nm* savouring; tasting

palanca *nf* (of meat) rib-eye; chuck steak

palangana *nf* [Colom] serving dish

paleta *nf* fish slice; spatula; [LatAm] ice lolly; [LatAm] (of beef) topside

paletería *nf* palate

paletilla *nf* shoulder

paleto *nm* deer

palillo *nm* toothpick; chopstick; stick

palito *nm* [Ar] ice lolly; **~ de pescado empanado** *nm* fishfinger; (of cinnamon) stick

pallar *nm* butter bean; [Andes, SCone] Lima bean

palma *nf* palm

palmatoria *nf* candlestick

palmiste *nm* palm oil

palmito *nm* [LatAm] palm heart

palo *nm* handle; stalk; **cuchara de ~** wooden spoon; **~ de amasar** [RPlate] rolling-pin; **regaliz de ~** stick of liquorice

paloma *nf* pigeon; **~ torcaz** wood pigeon

palometa *nf* sea fish: mackerel; moonfish; **~ de mar** [Ar] parona leatherjack

palomino *nm* young pigeon

palomita *nf* anisette/water drink; **~s de maíz** popcorn

palomo *a* pigeon

palote *nm* [Carib, SCone] rolling pin

palta *nf* [Andes, SCone] avocado pear

pámpana *nf* vine leaf

pampanito *nm* sea fish: sea chub

pámpano *nm* small bunch of grapes

pampear *vt* to roll out

pan *nm* bread, loaf; **~ de azúcar** sugar loaf; **~ blanco** (**~ candeal**) (**~ de flor**) white bread; **~ cenceño** unleavened bread; **~ de centeno** rye bread; **~ francés** [Ar] baguette; **~ integral** wholemeal loaf; **~ lactal** [Ar] sandwich loaf; **~ de molde** tin loaf; **~ moreno** brown loaf; **~ de Pascua** [Chile] panettoni; **~ rallado** breadcrumbs; **~ de higos** dried figs; **~ de jengibre** gingerbread; **fruto del ~** breadfruit; **~ de luche** seaweed; **~ del indio** mushroom: Indian's bread

pana *nf* [Chile] liver

panaché *nm* mixed salad

panadería *nf* bakery

panadero (a) *nm/f* baker

panamitos *nmpl* food; beans

panamos *nmpl* food, beans

panceta *nf* streaky bacon; uncured pork belly

pancho *nm* young sea-bream; [RPlate] hot-dog; **~ villa** [Chile] vegetable hash

pancita *nf* [Mex] tripe

pancito *nm* [LatAm] bread roll

panecillo *nm* bread roll

panela *nf* [Colom,Venez] hot lemon; **~ perra** [Chile] boiled water; [LatAm] brown sugar loaf

panera *nf* bread basket; bread bin

panil *nm* [SCone] celery

panita *nf* [Chile] liver

panizo *nm* millet; maize

panocha *nf* corncob; unrefined brown sugar; [Andes, CAmer, SCone] maize/cheese pancake; [Mex] molasses sweet

panque *nm* [Mex] sponge-cake

panqué *nm* [CAmer, Carib] pancake

panqueque *nf* [LatAm] pancake; **~ ruso** blini, caviar/sour-creamed pancake

panquequería *nf* [LatAm] pancake restaurant

pantorrilla *nf* (of leg) calf

panucho *nm* [Mex] stuffed tortilla

panul *nm* [SCone] celery

paño *nm* cloth; **~ de cocina**

dishcloth; **~ de los platos (~ de secar)** teacloth; **~ higiénico** [Spain] teacloth

papa *nf* potato; **~ dulce** sweet potato; **~ colchas** (potato) crisps; **~ fritas** chips, French fries; [Mex] porridge; [SCone] baby food

papalinas *nfpl* [CAmer] (potato) crisps

papandujo *a* [Spain] soft; overripe

papas *nfpl* [LatAm] mashed potato; [Chile] potatoes

papaya *nf* (of fruit) papaya

papel *nm* paper; **~ absorbente** kitchen paper; **~ (de) aluminio (~ de estaño)** aluminium/tin foil; **~ (de) arroz (~ de paja de arroz)** rice paper; **~ (de) grasa** greaseproof paper

papelillo *nm* cigarette; cigarette paper

papelón (ona) *nm/f* [Andes, Carib] sugar loaf

papero *a* [LatAm] potato

papilla *nf* baby food

papillote *nm* buttered paper; greased paper; **en ~** wrapped

paprika *nf* paprika

paquete *nm* (of cigarettes) packet; pack; (of flour/sugar &c) bag

par *nm* pair; two; couple; (of game) brace

paraguas *nm* mushroom

parasol *nm* parasol, sunshade

parchita *nf* [Carib] passion fruit

pareja *nf* pair; two; couple; (of game) brace

pargo *nm* snapper

parking (párking) *nm* car park

parlana *nf* [CAmer] turtle

parmesano *a* (of cheese) Parmesan

parqueadero *nm* [LatAm] car-park

parra *nf* vine

parral *nm* vineyard

parrilla *nf* grill; grillroom; steak restaurant

parrillada *nf* mixed grill; barbecue; [SCone] grill-room; steak restaurant

parte *nf* part

partenueces *nm* nutcracker

partir *vt* to cut; to break; to break off; to crack

party *nm* party; reception; cocktail party

pasa *nf* raisin; **~ corinto** currant; **~ de esmirna** saltana; **ciruela ~** prune

pasabocas *nmpl* [Colom] tasty mouthfuls; appetisers

pasado *a* (of bread) stale; (of fruit) overripe; (of meat) overdone; overcooked

pasador *nm* colander, sieve; strainer; filter

pasapalos *nmpl* [Mex, Venez] tasty mouthfuls; appetizers

pasaporte *nm* passport

pasapuré *nm* (of potato) masher; (of vegetables)

mincer

pasar *vt* to sieve; to strain; to filter; to pass; to place (in)

pasarse *vi* (of milk/fruit &c) to go off; (of solids) to get overcooked

pascana *nf* [Andes, SCone] inn

Pascua *nf* Christmas; Easter

pascualina *nf* [Ar, Urug] spinach/cheese quiche

pasmado *a* [LatAm] (of fruit) overripe

paso *a* (of fruit) dried; **ciruela ~** prune; **uva ~** raisin

pasoso *a* absorbent

pasta *nf* paste; pastry; pasta; dough; biscuit; **~ quebrada** shortcrust pastry; **~ de té** biscuits; **~ de anchoas/carne &c** anchovy/meat &c paste; **~ de verduras** thick vegetable soup

pastel *nm* cake; (of meat) pie; **~ de boda** wedding cake; **~ de crema** custard tart; **~ de cumpleaños** birthday cake; **~ de natillas** custard pie; [Chile] **~es** pâtisseries; **~ de papas** shepherd's/cottage pie

pastelado *nm* [Carib] choc-ice

pastelería *nf* pastries; cakes

pastelero *a* pastry; **~ rodillo** rolling-pin; pastry cook

pastelillo *nm* tart, **~ de hígado de ganso** [Spain] pâté de foie gras; [Spain] butter pat

pastelito *nm* [Ar] syrup-dipped sweet potato pasty

pasteurización *nf* pasteurization

pasteurizado *a* pasteurized

pasteurizar *vt* to pasteurize

pastilla *nf* (of chocolate) bar; piece; **~ de caldo** stock cube; **~ de fuego** firelighter; (of fruit) jujube

pastinaca *nf* parsnip

pasto *nm* food; (of wine) plonk

pastoso *a* doughy

pastura *nf* food

pata *nf* leg; (of pork) prime; **~ de cangrejo** crab-stick

pataca *nf* Jerusalem artichoke

patache *nm* [Andes] seafood soup; soup

patacón *nf* [Andes] fried banana

patasca *nf* [Andes] pork/maize stew

patata *nf* potato; **puré de ~s (~s deshechas)** mashed potatoes; **~s enteras** baked potatoes, jacket potatoes; **~ bravas** spicy tomato-sauced potatoes; **~ fritas** chips, French fries; (of packets) crisps; **~s nuevas** new potatoes

paté *nm* pâté

patilla *nf* [Carib] watermelon

patio *nm* patio

patita *nf* [Chile] (of pig) trotter

patí *nm* sea fish; pati

pato *nm* duck; **~ real (~ silvestre)** mallard

patriota *nm* [CAmer] banana

pava *nf* turkey; [SCone] kettle; maté pot

pavipollo *nm* young turkey

pavo (a) *nm/f* turkey; **de ~** [Chile] (of pasta) mushroom/cream/parmesan-ed

pebete *nm* [RPlate] bun

pebre *nm [esp* Chile] vinegar/tomato/garlic/parsley/onion/pepper sauce

pececillo *nm* minnow; small fresh water fish

pecera *nf* fishtank

pechina *nf* mollusc shell; scallop

pechuga *nf* (of chicken &c) breast

pectina *nf* pectin

pedazo *nm* piece; slice

pedido *nm* (of restaurant) order

pedir *vt* (of restaurant) to order

pedo *nm* **~ de monja** light pastry; **~ de lobo** mushroom: puffball

pedúnculo *nm* stalk

pegajoso *a* sticky

pegar *vt* to seal

peje *nm* fish; **~ araña** weever; **~ sapo** monkfish, angel shark

pejegallo *nm* sea fish: plownose chimera

pejeperro *nm* sea fish: red sheephead; hogfish

pejerrey de mar *nm* sea fish: whiting; silverside

pejesapo *nm* sea fish: clingfish

pejezorro *nm* sea fish: thresher shark

pela *nf* peeling

peladilla *nf* (of bean) Lima bean, [Spain] sugared almond; sea fish: peladilla

pelado *a* (of fruit/potato &c) peeled; (of peas/prawns &c) shelled; (of fowl) plucked; (of nuts &c) blanched

pelador *nm* [LatAm] peeler

peladura *nf* peeling; **~s** peel, peelings

pelágico *a* pelagic, deep-sea, open sea

pelambre *nm* skin

pelapatatas ([LatAm] **pelapapas)** *nm* potato peeler

pelar *vt* (of fruit) to peel; (of seafood) to shell; (of fowl) to pluck; to blanch; to peel after scalding; (of sweets) to unwrap

peleón ([LatAm] **peleonero)** *a* (of wine) plonk

pella *nf* lump; lump of fat; (of broccoli &c) head

pellejo *nf* skin; wineskin

pellingajo *nm* dishcloth

pellizcar *vt* to nibble

pellizco *nm* (of salt &c) pinch

pelón *nm* [RPlate] nectarine

pelotudo *a* [CAmer] (of sauce) lumpy

peltre *nm* pewter

peludo *nm* armadillo variety

penca *nf* prickly pear; [Mex] (of bananas) bunch; (of knife) blade

penedès *nm* spanish wine variety

peneque *nf* [Mex] stuffed tortilla

penga *nf* [Andes] bunch of bananas

pensión *nf* boarding-house; ~ **completa** full board; ~ **media** half-board

pepa *nf* [LatAm] (of fruit) pip; stone

pepián *nm* thick chili sauce; (of meat) thick chili sauced

pepinillo *nm* gherkin

pepino *nm* cucumber; ~ **de mar** sea cucumber

pepita *nf* pip; seed

pepito *nm* meat sandwich

pepitoria *nf* [Spain] (of chicken) white-sauce stewed with almonds; fricassée

peppermint *nm* crème de menthe

pequeño *a* small, little

pera *nf* pear; ~ **de agua** dessert pear

perbre *nm* [Chile] tomato/coriander/onion/chili dip

perca *nf* (of fish) perch

percebe *nm* barnacle

perdigón *nm* young partridge

perdiz *nf* partridge

perejil *nm* parsley

perfilarse *vi* to slim

perfume *nm* perfume; scent

perico *nm* asparagus; [Colom] white coffee; [Andes, Carib] scrambled eggs/fried onions

perifollo *nm* (of herb) chervil

pernil *nm* leg, [Carib] pork; leg of pork; haunch; upper leg; ham

perol *nm* saucepan; [Carib] kitchen utensil

perola *nf* saucepan

perrito caliente *nm* hot-dog

perro *nm* ~ **caliente** hot-dog; ~ **marino** dogfish; ~-**guía** guide-dog

peruana (a la) *nf* (of pisco sour) made with pica lemons

pervinca *nf* periwinkle

pesar *vt* to weigh

pesca *nf* fishing; ~ **de altura** deep-sea fishing; ~ **de bajura** coastal fishing; ~ **de arrastre** trawling

pescada *nf* hake

pescadería *nm* fish market; fishmonger

pescadilla *nf* sea fish: whiting; hake; striped weakfish

pescadito frito *nm* whitebait

pescado *nm* fish; ~ **magro (~ blanco)** whitefish; **cola de ~ (colapís) (colapiz)** isinglass

pescuezo *nm* neck

peso *nm* weight; scales

pestiño *nm* [Spain] honey-ed fritter

pesto *nm* pesto; pine-nut/garlic/parmesan/basil sauce

petaca *nf* hipflask; cigarette/cigar case; tobacco pouch

petisú *nm* cream puff

pez *nm* fish; ~ **sierra** sawfish;

~ espada swordfish; **~ de río** freshwater fish; **~ martillo** sea fish: hammerhead; **~ volador** flying fish; **~ limón** yellowtail amberjack

piamontés *a* (of salad) from Piedmont

pibil *nm* [Mex] chili sauce

picada *nf* spicy sauce; [SCone] tapas; appetisers; snacks; [SCone] small restaurant

picadillo *nm* (of meat) mince; (of vegetable) finely-chopped dish

picado *a* chopped; (of meat) minced; (of wine) off

picadora *nf* [Spain, RPlate] (of meat) mincer

picana *nf* [SCone] (of meat) haunch

picante *a* spicy, hot; (of wine) off; *nm* chili; [SCone, Andes] chili-ed meat stew

picantería *nf* [Andes, SCone] (of spicy foods) economy restaurant

picantón *nm* spicy sauce

picar *vt/vi* to nibble (at); to chop; [SCone] to mince; (of vegetables/wine &c) to go off; to be spicy; (of ice) to crush

picarón *nm* [LatAm] fritter; doughnut

picatoste *nm* fried bread; croûton

pichanga *nf* [Chile] diced ham/cheese/gherkin; [SCone] cocktail tit-bits

piche *nm* (of milk) whey; [SCone] armadillo

pichel *nm* mug; [Mex] pitcher

pichintún *nm* smidgin; tiny bit

pichón *nm* young pigeon; [LatAm] chick

pichuncho *nm* pisco/Martini® aperitif

pickles *nmpl* [SCone] pickles

picnic *nm* picnic; picnic basket

pico *nm* (of jug) spout

picoroco *nm* crustacean: giant barnacle

picoso *a* very hot; spicy

picota *nf* bigarreau cherry

picotear *vt* (of eating) to pick at

picuda *nf* woodcock; barracuda

picure *nm* [Carib] spicy sauce

pie *nm* **~s de cerdo** (pig's) trotters; (of glass &c) foot, base, stem, bottom; (of plant) stem; [Chile] filled pastry-case

piedra (en) *nf* [SCone] hot sauce

piel *nf* skin; peel; (of potatoes) jacket

pierna *nf* lamb/mutton/pork leg

pieza *nf* (of fruit/meat/dinner service &c) piece

pil pil *nm* (of fish) **al ~** oil-cooked

pila *nf* (of kitchen) sink

pilche *nm* gourd

pildorita *nf* [SCone] cocktail sausage

pileta *nf* (of kitchen) sink; [Chile] drinking fountain; [RPlate] swimming pool

pilón *nm* sugar loaf

piloncillo *nm* fine brown sugar

pilsen ([Chile] **pílsener)** *nf* beer

piltrafa *nf* (of meal) scrap

pimentero *nm* pepperpot

pimentón *nm* paprika, ~ **picante** cayenne pepper); [LatAm] sweet pepper, capsicum

pimienta *nf* (of condiment) pepper; ~ **de cayena** cayenne pepper; ~ **inglesa** allspice

pimiento *nm* (of vegetable) pepper; ~ **del piquillo (~ morrón) (~ rojo)** red pepper; ~ **verde** green pepper

pinchar *vt* (of cooking) to test; (of fruit &c) to prick; to pierce

pinche *nm/f* kitchen worker

pinchito *nm* [Spain] tapa

pincho *nm* tapa; small piece; ~ **moruno** pork kebab

pino *nm* [Chile] beef/onion fried mince; mince

pinol(e) *nm* [CAmer, Mex] roasted maize or cornflour drink

pinolillo *nm* maize flour; (of drink) maize flour

pinta *nf* pint; (of drink) drop

pintada *nf* guinea-fowl

pintado *a* (of coffee) with drop of milk; *nm* [Spain] wine/ vermouth cocktail

pintar *vt* to coat; (of fruit &c) to ripen

pintarroja *nf* dogfish

pinto *a* (of bean) pinto; (of fruit) right colour

pinza *nf* (of crab &c) pincer; claw; ~**s** (of sugar) tongs

piña *nf* pineapple

piñata *nf* festival sweets-container

piñón *nm* pine nut

piñonate *nm* sugared pine-nut

piola *nf* agave

pipa *nf* (of wine) barrel; (of plant) seed; sunflower seed; [Andes] green coconut

pipas *nfpl* seeds

pipeño *nm* (of wine) Chilean white

pipián *nm* squash variety; (of sauce) thick chili; chili-sauced meat

pipote *nm* cask

piquete *nm* [Andes] picnic; (of liquid) drop

pirá pitá *nf* [Ar] freshwater fish: pirá pitá

pirámide *nf* pyramid

piraya (piraña) *nf* sea fish: piranha

piré *nm* [Venez] mashed potato

Pirineo *a* of the Pyrenees

pirucho *nm* [CAmer] (of ice-cream) cornet

piruleta *nf* lollipop

pirulí *nm* lollipop

pisar *vt* to squeeze; (of grapes) to tread

piscifactoría *nf* fish farm

piscigranaja *nf* [LatAm] fish farm

piscina *nf* swimming-pool

pisco *nm* [Chile, Peru] the national (grape) spirits drink; ~ **sour (saur) (sauer)** [Chile, Peru] pisco/lemon cocktail; [Andes] turkey

piscola *nm* [Chile] (of long drink) pisco/cola

piscolabis *nm* snack

piso *nm* (of level) floor

pistacho *nm* pistachio

pisto *nm* ratatouille; (of chicken) broth

pistola *nf* (of bread) baguette

pistón *nm* [CAmer, Mex] corn tortilla

pita *nf* (of salt &c) pinch; (of plant) agave

pitilla *nf* [SCone] string

pitillo *nm* [Andes, Carib] (of drinking) straw

pito de ternera *nm* [LatAm] steak sandwich

piure *nm* [Chile] Chilean pyurid

pixtón *nm* [CAmer] thick tortilla

pizca *nf* (of salt &c) pinch; (of liquid) drop

pizza *nf* pizza

pizzería *nf* pizzeria

pizzeta *nf* small pizza

pla de bages *nm* spanish wine variety

placaminero *nm* persimmon

plaga *nf* glut

plancha *nf* grill; griddle; [SCone] griddle pan; **a la** ~ grilled

planchado *a* pressed

planta *nf* plant

plata *nf* silverware

Plata (la) *nf* River Plate

platacho *nm* [SCone] raw seafood dish

platada *nf* [LatAm] plateful; dish

platanero *a* banana

plátano *nm* banana

plateada *nf* [Chile] meatcut between ribs and outer fat; flank

platería *nf* silverware; silver

platija *nf* (of fish) flounder; plaice; lemon sole; flat fish variety

platilla *nf* water melon

platillo *nm* saucer; small plate; [CAmer, Mex] (of menu) course

plato *nm* (of crockery) plate; (of menu) course; dish; ~ **de postre** dessert plate; ~ **frutero** fruit bowl; ~ **hondo** (~ **sopero**) soup plate; ~ **llano** dinner plate; ~ **del día** dish of the day; ~ **dulce** pudding course; ~ **fuerte (~ principal)** main course; ~ **combinado** set main course; (of recipe) dish; different ingredients on same plate

platón *nm* serving dish

playa *nf* beach

plaza *nf* aperitif: beer

pluma *nf* feather

pluscafé *nm* [LatAm] post-prandial liqueur

pobre *nmf* **patatas a la** ~ paupers' potatoes; fried egg/

potatoes/onions/peppers dish

poch(e)ar *vt* to poach

pocha *nf* haricot bean

pocho *a* (of fruit) overripe, soft

pochoclo *nm* [Ar] popcorn

pocillo *nm* mug, small earthenware dish/bowl; [LatAm] coffee cup; [Mex] tankard

poco *a* little; **un ~** a bit, a little; few

polaco *a* Catalan

poleada *nf* [CAmer] hot milk/ flour drink

polenta *nf* [Andes, SCone] cornflour; polenta, ground maize

polla *nf* pullet

pollino (a) *nm/f* donkey

pollito (polluelo) *nm* chick

pollo *nm* chicken

polo *nm* ice lolly

polvillo *nm* (of rice) bran

polvo *nm* powder; **~ de hornear** baking powder

polvorear *vt* to dust (with); to powder; to sprinkle (with)

polvorón *nm* shortbread

poma *nf* apple; [Andes] carafe

pomelo *nm* grapefruit

ponchada *nf* bowl of punch

ponche *nm* punch; mulled wine; **~ de huevo** eggnog

ponchera *nf* punch bowl

poner *vt* to put; to add; *vi* (of fowl) to lay (eggs); **poner los manteles (~ la mesa)** to lay the table

ponqué *nm* [Venez, Col] cake, tart

pop *nm* popcorn

popote *nm* [Mex] drinking straw

popurrí *nm* potpourri

poquísimo *a* very little

poquitín *nm* little bit

poquito *nm* **un ~** a little bit; drop

porcelana *nf* porcelain, china

porcino *a* pig, porcine

porción *nf* piece; portion; (of cake &c) slice

porcuno *a* pig

poro *nm* [LatAm] leek

porongo *nm* [LatAm] gourd, calabash

pororó *a* [SCone] popcorn

porotito *nm* bean variety

poroto *nm* [Andes, SCone] bean; **~ verde** runner bean

porra *nf* large fritter; cooking pot

porrón *nm* (of wine) long spouted drinking jar; [Ar] bottle of beer; [SCone] leek; green pepper

portabebés *nm* carrycot

portabotellas *nm* wine rack

portacheques *nm* chequebook

portacubiertos *nm* cutlery tray

portatostadas *nm* toast-rack

posada *nf* [CAmer, Mex] Christmas party

posadero (a) *nm/f* innkeeper

posafuentes *nmpl* [SCone] tablemat; trivet

posavasos *nm* coaster

poso *nm* sediment; lees; dregs;

posta *nf* slice; **~ de pierna** (CAmer) (of pork) leg

postol *nm* [CAmer] maize drink

postre *nm* dessert; **~s** afters

pota *nf* cuttlefish

potable *a* drinkable; (of water) drinking; (of meal) edible

potaje *nm* vegetable/pulse stew

pote *nm* jar, jug; [Venez] tin; [Mex] mug; [Andes, Carib] flask

potente *a* [Chile] (of sauce) hot

poto *nm* earthenware jug; gourd

potrillo *nm* [Chile] tall glass

poyo *nm* (of kitchen) stone worktop

pozo *nm* (of water) well; **~ artesiano** artesian well

pozole *nm* [Mex] maize stew

praliné *nm* praline

precio *nm* price; charge

precocinado *a* pre-cooked

precocinar *vt* to pre-cook

prefrito *a* pre-fried

premio *nm* prize

prendedera *nf* [Andes] waitress

prensaajos *nm* garlic crusher

prensalimones *nm* lemon-squeezer

preparado *a* ready-cooked

preparar *vt* (of meal &c) to prepare; to make

presa *nf* (of meat) piece; (of bird) claw

presentación *nf* (of dish) presentation

presión *nf* (of saucepan) pressure-cooker; (of beer) draught beer

presurizado *a* pressurized

prieta *nf* [SCone] black pudding; blood sausage

primavera *nf* (of season) spring

primero *a* first; top quality; early

primicia *nf* first fruit

principale *a* (of course) main

principio *nm* entrée

pringada *nf* dunked bread

pringar *vt* (of bread) to dunk; to dip; (of roast) to baste

pringo *nm* [LatAm] (of liquid) drop; (of salt &c) pinch

pringue *nm* juices; sauce; dripping

priorato *nm* spanish wine variety

prisco *nm* apricot; peach variety

probar *vt* to sample, to taste, to try; (of allergic substance) to [not] agree with

promoción *nf* promotion; special offer

pronto *adv* quickly; soon; early; [SCone] (of meal &c) ready

prontuario *nm* guide; handbook

propietario (a) *nm/f* proprietor

propina *nf* tip, gratuity

propio *a* own

proscrito (proscripto [Arg]) *a*

banned, disallowed

proteico (proteínico) *a* protein

proteína *nf* protein

provecho *nm* (of meal) ¡**buen ~!** Enjoy your meal! Bon appétit!

proveedor (dora) *nm/f* purveyor

provenzal *a* provençal

provocativo *a* appetising; mouth-watering

provolone *a* (of cheese) grana padona

próximo *a* next

prueba *nf* trying, sampling, testing; taste, sample

pub *nm* bar with music

pucha *nf* [Mex] (of bread) ring-shaped loaf

puchera *nf* stew

puchero *nm* cooking pot; beef/mutton/sausage/vegetables stew

puches *nmpl* porridge

puco *nm* [Andes, SCone] earthenware bowl

pudín *nm* pudding; **~ de pan y mantequilla** bread-and-butter pudding

puerco (a) *nm/f* pig (sow); **~ jabalí** wild boar; **~ de mar** porpoise

puerro *nm* leek

puerta *nf* door; **~ cortafuegos** fire door; **~ giratoria** revolving door; **~ oscilante** swing door

puesto *nm* stall; kiosk

pulique *nm* [CAmer] chili/maize dish

pulmón *nm* lung; lights

pulpa *nf* (of fruit) flesh; (of meat) fillet

pulpejo *nm* fleshypart; soft part

pulpería *nf* tavern

pulpo *nm* octopus

pulposo *a* pulpy; fleshy

pulque *nf* [Mex] (of drink) pulque; fermented maguey (agave) drink

pulquería *nf* [Mex] bar

punches *nmpl* [CAmer] popcorn

punta *nf* (of knife) tip; (of salt) pinch; **~s de espárrago** asparagus tips; **~s de carne** finest cuts of meat; (of tobacco) finest; (of table) end

puntal *nm* [LatAm] snack

puntita *nf* (of salt &c) small pinch

punto *nm* point; (of freezing/boiling/melting/maturity &c) **a ~** at the point of; just right; (of meat) medium rare; [SCone] (of coffee) with alcohol; (of fruit) ripe

pupurrí *nm* pot-pourri

pupusa *nf* [CAmer] stuffed tortilla

puré *nm* purée; thick soup; **~ de patatas** mashed potatoes; **~ de tomate** tomato purée; **~ de verduras** vegetable soup; **~ bravas** spicy tomato-sauced fried potatoes

puro *nm* cigar, **~ habano** Havana cigar

purrela *nf* (of wine) plonk
puye *nm* sea fish: peladilla
puzcua *nf* [Mex] puffed maize

Q

Quáker® *nm* [LatAm] porridge
quebradizo *a* (of pastry) shortcrust; crumbly
queimada *nf* flamed orujo(marc)/sugar/lemon drink
queja *nf* complaint
quelite *nm* [CAmer, Mex] greens
quelonia *nf* [Carib] turtle
queltehues *nm* [Chile] game bird: teruteru
quemado *a* burnt
quemador *nm* burner
quemar *vi* to be boiling hot; *vt* to burn; to scald
queque *nm* [LatAm] cake
quequito *nm* [Lat Am] small cake
querer *vt* to like; to want
quesadilla *nf* cheesecake; [LatAm] folded stuffed maize tortilla; pasty
quesera *nf* cheese dish
quesería *nf* cheeses; dairy produce
quesero *a* cheese
quesillo *nm* [CAmer] fresh cheese-filled tortilla; [Andes] curd; cheese; [Venez] crème caramel
queso *nm* cheese; ~ **azul** blue cheese; ~ **de bola** Edam; ~

crema (~ **de nata**) [LatAm] cream cheese; ~ **fresco** green cheese; ~ **fundido** processed cheese; ~ **manchego** ewe's milk cheese of La Mancha; ~ **de mano** [Venez] mozzarella-type cheese; ~ **mantecoso** soft cheese; ~ **de oveja** ewe's milk cheese; ~ **parmesano** Parmesan cheese; ~ **rallado** grated cheese; ~ **de untar** cheese spread; ~ **helado** ice-cream brick; ~ **de puerco** (~ **de cerdo**) (~ **de cabeza**) [Mex] jellied pork, brawn
quey *nm* [Andes] cake
quiche *nm* quiche
quilo (**kilo**) *nm* kilogramme
quina *nf* quinine; (of wine) tonic wine
quincho *nm* [SCone] (of restaurant) steak-house
quinina *nf* quinine
quinto *nm* (of beer) small bottle
quiosco *nm* kiosk; ~ **de nescesidad** public WC
quirquincho *nm* armadillo variety
quisquilla *nf* shrimp
quitapenas *nm* stiff drink
quitar *vt* (of skin &c) to remove; ~ **la mesa** to clear the table
quitasol *nm* sunshade, parasol
quitón (**apretador**) (**chitón**) *nm* mollusc variety

R

raba *nf* squid (calamari) rings

rabada *nf* rump

rabadilla *nf* (of poultry) parson's nose; pope's nose; (of cattle) rump

rabanada *nf* (of bread) slice

rábano *nm* radish, ~ **picante** horseradish; **salsa de ~** horseradish sauce

rabillo *nm* stalk; stem

rabo *nm* stalk; stem; (of animal) tail; ~ **de buey** oxtail

racimo *nm* (of cauliflower &c) branch; cluster

ración *nf* portion

racionar *vt* to share out

radiotaxi *nm* radio taxi

raíz *nf* root

raja *nf* slice, ~**s** [Mex] pickled green pepper

rajita *nf* thin slice

rale *nm* [SCone] wooden bowl

rallado *a* grated; (of bread) breadcrumbs

rallador *nm* grater

ralladura de limón *nf* grated lemon rind

rallar *vt* to grate

rallo *nm* grater

rama *nf* sprig; stick

ramillete *nm* (of flowers) bunch, bouquet; ~ **guarnecido** bouquet garni

ramita *nf* sprig

rana *nf* frog; ~ **toro** bullfrog

ranchear *vi* [Andes, SCone] to have a meal

ranchero *a* **huevos ~s** chili/tomato sauced fried eggs

rancho *nm* communal meal

ranciedad (rancidez) *nf* (of perishables) rancid-ness, staleness; (of wine) age, maturity, mellowness

rancio *a* (of wine) old, mellow; (of butter &c) rancid

rapadura *nf* [LatAm] brown sugar; milk/syrup sweet

rape *nm* sea fish: angler fish, monkfish; [USA] goosefish

rapido *a* quick

rasado *a* level; up to brim

rascacio *nm* sea fish: scorpion fish

raseado *a* (of spoonful &c) level

rasera *nf* fish slice

raso *a* level; level with the brim

raspa *nf* fishbone; backbone; [Carib, Mex] brown sugar; (of fruit) stalk

raspado *a* water ice

raspador *nm* [Mex] grater

raspadura *nf* [LatAm] brown sugar

raspar *vt* to be rough (on throat &c); to scrape; to crush; to grate

rastrillazo *nm* snack

rastro *nm* abattoir

rato *nm* period; time

ravioles *nmpl* ravioli

ravioli *nmpl* ravioli

raya *nf* sea fish: skate, ray

real *a* royal

reaprovisionar *vt* to restock

rebaja *nf* discount

rebajar *vt* to dilute; (of price) to reduce; to discount

rebanada *nf* slice

rebanar *vt* to slice

rebañar *vt* (of platter) to mop clean [with bread]

rebojo *nm* crust

reborde *nm* rim; edge

rebosante *a* brimming with

rebosar *vi* (of liquid) to overflow; (of harvest) to be in abundance

rebozado *a* battered/ breadcrumbed

rebozar *vt* to batter/breadcrumb

rebullir *vt* (of tea &c) to stir

rebusca *nf* gleanings

recado *nm* message; shopping

recalentado *a* reheated

recalentar *vt* to reheat; to heat up; to warm up

recaudo *nm* [LatAm] condiments; spices; fresh vegetables

recepción *nf* (of a function) reception

recepcionista *nm/f* receptionist

receta *nf* recipe

recetario *nm* recipe book

rechinado *a* [CAmer, Mex] overcooked

recibimiento *nm* reception; welcome

recibir *vt* to welcome

recibo *nm* receipt; bill

reciclar *vt* to recycle

recocer *vt* to heat up; to warm up; [SCone] to cook

recocido *a* overdone; overcooked

recocina *nf* scullery

recoger la mesa *vt* to clear the table

recogida *nf* harvest

recolección *nf* harvest

recomendación *nf* recommendation

recomendar *vt* (of restaurant) to recommend

recova *nf* [SCone] food market

rectificar *vt* (of sugar &c) to adjust; to add

recubierto *a* covered; topped

recubrir *vt* to coat; to cover; to top

red *nf* (of sieve) mesh

redoma *nf* flask

redondo *nm* rump steak

redrojo *nm* late fruit

reducción *nf* (of sauce) thickening

reducir *vt* to reduce; to boil down; (of sauce) to thicken

refacción *nf* snack

refectorio *nm* refectory

refractario *a* ovenproof

refregar *vt* to rub; to clean

refrescarse *vi* (of drink) to have one; [Andes] to take tea

refresco *nm* soft drink

refresquería *nf* refreshment stall

refri *nm* [Mex] fridge

refrigeración *nf* refrigeration; air conditioning

refrigerado *a* (of food) chilled; (of room) air conditioned; (of liquids) cold

refrigerador *nm* fridge

refrigeradora *nf* [LatAm] fridge

refrigerar *vt* to chill; to refrigerate

refrigerio *nm* cool drink; snack

refrito *a* rehashed; *nm* hash; fry-up

refuerzo *nm* [Urug] baguette sandwich

regaliz *nm* (**regaliza** *nf*) liquorice; ~ **de palo** stick of liquorice

regalo *nm* gift

regar *vt* to baste

régimen *nm* diet, ~ **de adelgazamiento** slimming diet

región *nf* region

regional *a* regional; from the region

regular *a* (of oven heat) medium; (of size) medium; average

regustar *vt* [Carib, Mex] to taste, to savour

regusto *nm* aftertaste

rehogar *vt* to sauté; (of vegetables) to sweat; to lightly fry

reina claudia *nf* greengage

reineta (**rey nata**) *nf* pippin; sea fish: Atlantic pomfret

rejilla *nf* (of oven) shelf; [SCone] meat-safe

rejita *nf* slice

rejudo *a* sticky; [Carib] (of liquid) runny

relajante *a* [SCone] sticky-sweet

rellena *nf* [Mex, Col] black pudding

rellenar *vt* to stuff

relleno *a* stuffed; *nm* stuffing; filling

reloj de estacionamiento *nm* parking meter

reluciente *a* well-fed

remaduro *a* [LatAm] overripe

remojar *vt* to soak; to dunk

remojón *nm* (of bread) soaked in milk

remolacha *nf* beetroot; ~ **azucarera** sugar beet

remoreno *nm* sea fish: rainbow runner; prodigal son

remover *vt* (of liquids &c) to stir; (of salad &c) to toss

reno *nm* reindeer

renuevo *nm* shoot; sprout

reo *nm* sea trout

reparado *a* (of meal) fortifying

repartidor (a) *nm/f* (of pizzas &c) delivery person

repasador *nm* [SCone] dishcloth

repasar *vt* [SCone] to wipe

repe *nm* [Andes] mashed bananas/milk

repetir *vt* to repeat; *vi* (of helping of food) to have more; to have seconds; (of drink) to top-up; to have another one

repollito de bruselas *nm* brussels sprouts

repollo *nm* cabbage; [SCone] ~ **morado (~ colorado)** red cabbage

reposaplatos *nm* table mat

repostería *nf* larder; (of shop) confectioner's; (of pastry) baking

repostero (a) *nm/f* pastry cook; [Andes] larder; kitchen shelf

repuesto *nm* (of furniture) sideboard

repulgar *vt* (of pastry) to pattern the edge

repulgo *nm* (of pastry) patterned edge

repuntarse *vpr* (of perishables) to turn

requemado *a* (of dish) overdone

requemar (resquemar) *vt* to burn

requera *nm* Spanish wine variety

requesón *nm* cottage cheese

res *nf* [Mex] steak; [LatAm] (of meat) beef

resaca *nf* well-made spirits

resacado *nm* [Andes] hooch

rescoldo *nm* (of barbecue &c) hot ashes

reseco *a* (of bread &c) dry

reserva *nm* vintage wine (minimum three years old); (of table) reservation, booking

reservación *nf* [LatAm] reservation

reservado *nm* (of restaurant) private room; [SCone] (of wine) vintage wine

reservar *vt* (of restaurant table) to reserve, to book

resguardo de consigna *nm* cloakroom ticket

resquemar (requemar) *vt* to burn

resquemor *nm* burnt taste

restauración *nf* restaurant trade

restaurador (a) *nm/f* restaurant owner

restaurante (restaurant) (restaurán) (restorán) *nm* restaurant

restos *nmpl* left-overs

retobado *a* [LatAmer] (of animal) wild

retoño *nm* shoot; sprout

retornable *a* (of bottle &c) returnable

retostar *nm* to overcook; to burn

retrasarse *vpr* to be late

retrete *nm* WC, toilet

reunión *nf* reunion; gathering; meeting

reutilizable *a* re-usable

reutilización *nf* re-use; recycling

revenirse *vpr* (of bread/fruit &c) to go stale; (of wine) to go off; to become corked

revés *nm* other side; reverse;

back

revoltijo (revoltillo) *nm* (of food/drink) concoction; ~ **de huevos** scrambled eggs

revoltura (revuelto *nm*) *nf* scrambled eggs/vegetable dish

revolver *vt* to stir; to mix; to shake; (of salad) to toss

revuelto *a* (of eggs) scrambled; *nm* **(revoltura** *nf*) scrambled eggs/vegetable dish; ~ **de gambas** scrambled eggs/prawns dish; [Andes] grape juice; must

rías baixas *nm* spanish wine variety

ribeira del duero *nm* spanish wine variety

ribeira del guadiana *nm* spanish wine variety

ribeira sacra *nm* spanish wine variety

ribeiro *nm* Galician young white wine

riboflavina *nf* vitamin B; riboflavin

rico *a* delicious; lovely; tasty

ricota *nf* ricotta; cow, goat or ewe soft white cheese

rigue *nm* [CAmer] tortilla

rijoso *nf* gristle

riñón *nm* kidney

riñonada *nf* kidney stew; loin

río *nm* river

rioja *nm* Spanish wine variety

rioplatense *a* of the River Plate

ripiar *vt* to crumble; [Carib, Andes] to shred

risotto *nm* risotto

ristra *nf* (of onions &c) string

rizado *a* curly; (of cabbage) curly kale

robalo (róbalo) *nm* sea bass; [Chile] mullet; [Ar] patagonian blenny

rociar *vt* (of swallowing) to rinse down; to sprinkle; to baste

rochancho *nm* sea fish: Lorna drum

rococo *nm* sea fish: drum; croaker

rocote (rocoto) *nm* [LatAm] large pepper; large chili

rodaballo *nm* sea fish: turbot; ~ **menor** sea fish: brill

rodaja *nf* slice

Ródano *nm* Rhône

rodillo *nm* rolling pin

rojo *a* red

rollito *nm* roll; ~ **de primavera** spring roll

rollizo *nm* sea fish: sand-perch

rollo *nm* [Spain] rolling pin; pastry roll, ~ **de primavera** spring roll

romana (a la) *a* (of fish) battered

romaza *nf* sorrel

romero *nm* (of herb) rosemary

rompenueces *nm* nutcrackers

romper *vt* to break

rompope *nm* [CAmer, Mex] eggnog

ron *nm* rum

roncha *nf* slice

ropa vieja *nf* meat stew

roquefort *a* (of cheese) roquefort

rorcual *nm* finback whale

rosado *nm* rosé wine

rosbif *nm* roast beef

rosca (rosco *nm*) *nf* ring-shaped bread roll/pastry; doughnut

roscón *nm* ring-shaped cake

rosetas (rositas) *nfpl* popcorn

rosquilla *nf* ring-shaped pastry; doughnut

rostizado *a* roast

rostizar *vt* to spit-roast

rotar *vt* to roast

rucho *a* [Andes] (of fruit) overripe

rueda *nf* slice; sea fish: sunfish; spanish wine variety

ruibarbo *nm* rhubarb

rulo *nm* rolling pin

ruso *a* (of salad &c) russian

rustidera *nf* roasting tin

S

sábado *nm/adv* Saturday; ~ **de Gloria (Santa)** Easter Saturday

sábalo *nm* sea fish: shad

saber *vi* to taste

sabor *nm* savour; taste; **sin ~** flavourless; tasteless

saborcillo *nm* slight taste

saborear *vt* (of dish) to taste; to savour; (of preparation) to flavour

saborete *nm* slight taste

saborizante *nm* flavouring

sabrosera *nf* titbit; appetizer

sabroso *a* tasty, delicious; meaty; tasty; juicy

sabrosón (sona) *a* (of fruit) delicious

sacacorchos *nm* corkscrew

sacar *vt* to remove

sacarina (sacarino *nm*) *nf* saccharin(e)

saciar *vt* (of hunger) to assuage; to satisfy; (of thirst) to quench

saciedad (hasta) *nf* (of eating/ drinking) to one's fill

saín *nm* (of animal) fat

sainete *nm* seasoning; sauce; delicacy; appetizer

sal *nf* salt; ~ **gema** rock salt; ~ **marina** sea salt; ~ **común** (~ **de cocina) (~ gorda) (~ gruesa)** cooking salt; ~ **de mesa** (~ **fina)** table salt

sala *nf* room; ~ **de espera** waiting-room; ~ **de fumadores** smoking room, ~ **de té** tearoom

saladito *nm* [SCone] bar snack

salado *a* salted; salty; savoury

salame (salami) *nm* salami

salar *vt* to salt

salazón *nf* salted meat/fish

salbute *nm* [Mex] stuffed tortilla

salchicha *nf* sausage; ~ **de Frankfurt** *nm* frankfurter

salchichón *nm* salami sausage

variety

salchipapa *nf* [Andes] kebab variety

salcochar *vt* to cook in salted water

salero *nm* salt cellar

salida *nf* way-out, exit; **~ de emergencia** emergency exit; **~ de incendios** fire exit

salinizarse *vpr* to become salty

salirse *vpr* (of liquid) to leak out; to boil over; to overflow

salivadera *nf* spittoon

salmi *nm* wine stew

salmón *nm* salmon; **~ encerrado** [Ar] landlocked salmon; **~ del pacífico** chinook salmon

salmonela *nf* salmonella

salmonete *nm* sea fish: red mullet

salmuera *nf* pickle, brine

salón *nm* room; reception room

salonero *nm* [Andes] waiter

salpicón *nm* seafood or meat onion/tomato/peppers salad-ed; cold mixed fruit juice; [Andes, SCone] raw vegetable salad; fruit juice cocktail

salpimentar *vt* (of salt/pepper) to season

salpreso *a* salted

salsa *nf* sauce, relish; (of meat) gravy; (of salad) dressing; **~ americana** thousand island dressing; tomato/ketchup/mayonnaise sauce; **~ china** soya sauce; **~ holandesa** hollandaise sauce; **~ inglesa** worcestershire sauce; **~ mayonesa (~ mahonesa)** mayonnaise; **~ tartara** tartar sauce; **~ verde** parsley sauce

salsera *nf* sauce boat

salteado *a* sautéd

saltear *vt* to sauté; to sweat

salteña *nf* [Andes] meat pie

saltón *a* [LatAm] undercooked

¡salucita! *excl* [LatAm] Your health! Cheers!

¡salud! *excl* Your health! Cheers!

salva *nf* salver; tray

salvado *nm* bran

salvaje *a* (of fruit/animal) wild

salvajino *a* wild; (of meat) game

salvamanteles *nm* table mat

salvaplatos *nm* table mat

salvia *nf* sage

salvilla *nf* [SCone] cruet; salver; tray

sambumbia *nf* [CAmer, Carib, Mex] fruit drink; [Mex] (of drink) pineapple; barley water

san pedro *nm* [Chile] nutty whisky vanilla ice-cream

sancho *nm* pig; [Mex] ram; lamb; goat

sancochar *vt* to parboil

sancocho *nm* (of food) undercooking; (of meat) parboiling; [LatAm] meat or fish/plantain &c stew

sandía *nf* watermelon

sánduche *nm* [LatAm]

sandwich

sándwich *nm* sandwich

sandwichera *nf* toasted-sandwich maker

sandwichería *nf* sandwich bar

sango *nm* [Andes] yucca/maize pudding

sangre *nf* blood

sangría *nf* sangria; red wine/lemonade/fruit drink

sánguche (sanguchito) *nm* [LatAm] sandwich

sangüich *nm* [Spain] sandwich

sanguinolento *a* (of meat) rare, underdone

sanitario *nm* [Mex, Venez, Colom] WC, toilet

sanjacobo *nm* cheesed escalope

sano *a* of good quality; healthy; wholesome

santo *nm* saint's day; name day

sapo (peje) *a* (of sea fish) monkfish, angel shark; *nm* toad

saque *nm* appetite

saquito *nm* small bag

sardina *nf* sardine; pilchard; sprat; ~ **arenque** herring

sardinero *a* sardine

sardineta *nf* sprat

sargo *nm* sea fish: coquito sergeant; bream

sarrio *nm* goat variety

sarro *nm* (of kettle) scale

sarta *nf* string

sartén *nf* frying pan

sasafrás *nm* sassafras

satsuma *nf* satsuma

saturado *a* saturated

saúco *nm* elder; **baya del ~** elderberry

sazón *a* [Andes, CAmer, Mex] ripe

sazón *nf* ripeness; seasoning; **fuera de ~** out of season; flavour

sazonado *a* (of fruit) ripe; (of dish) seasoned; flavoured

sazonar *vt* (of fruit) to ripen; (of dish) ~ **de** to season with; to spice

schop *nm* [SCone] tankard; beer; draught beer

sebo *nm* suet

secado al sol *a* sun-dried

secador *nm* teacloth

secar *vt* to dry; **paño de ~** tea towel

seco *a* (of wine &c) dry; [Colom] main course

sed *nf* thirst; **tener ~** to be thirsty

seibó *nm* [Andes, Venez] sideboard

seis *a* six

selección *nf* selection

seleccionado *a* chosen; selected

selecto *a* (of wine) select

self-service *nm* (of restaurant) self-service

seltz (agua (de)) *nm* seltzer, soda water

selva negra *a* (of cake) black-forest

semana *nf* week

semicurado *a* half-cured

semidesnatado (semi-descremado) *a* semi-skimmed

semilla *nf* seed; (of fruit) **sin ~s** seedless

semi-seco *a/nm* medium-dry

semivacío *a* half empty

sémola *nf* semolina; **~ de arroz** ground rice

sensación *nf* sensation

sensitiva *nf* mimosa

sentada *nf* (of restaurant) sitting

sentar *vt* to seat; to sit (someone)

sentarse *vpr* to sit down

señor (a) *nm/f* waiter (waitress)

señorita *nf* (of young lady) waitress

separar *vt* (of ingredients &c) to set aside; to divide; to detach; to remove

sepia *nf* cuttlefish

septiembre *nm* September

serba *nf* rowanberry

serpiente *nm* snake

serpol *nm* wild thyme

serrano *a* (of ham) Parma

servicio *nm* service, set; **~ de café** coffee set/service; **~ de mesa** dinner service; **~ de té** tea set/service; WC, toilet

servilleta *nf* napkin; serviette

servilletero *nm* napkin ring, serviette ring

servir *vt* to serve; (of drink) to pour

sésamo *nm* sesame

sesos *nmpl* brains

seta *nf* mushroom; boletus mushroom

setero *a* mushroom

setiembre *nm* September

seviche (cebiche) *nm* hors d'oeuvre raw fish/shellfish dish

siberita *nm* epicure, gourmet

sidra *nf* cider

sidrero *a* cider

sidrina *nf* cider

sierpe *nf* snake

sierra *nf* [Mex] swordfish; snock

siesta *nf* siesta, nap

siete *a* seven; seventh

sifón *nm* syphon; **whisky con ~** whisky and soda; [Andes] bottled beer

siglo *nm* century, age

silla *nf* seat, chair; **~ alta** high chair; **~ de ruedas** wheelchair

sillón *nm* armchair; easy chair; **~ de ruedas** wheelchair

siluro *nm* catfish

silvestre *a* wild

simiente *nf* seed

simple *a* simple; plain

sin *prep* without; **~ alcohol** non-alcoholic; **~ gas** (of drink) still; **~ hueso** boneless; (of tax/service &c) not including

siró *nm* [Carib] syrup

sirope *nm* [LatAm] syrup

smoking *nm* dinner jacket, tuxedo

snack *nm* snack; snack bar

soasar *vt* to lightly roast

sobao *nm* sponge cake

sobrados *nmpl* [SCone] left-overs

sobras *nfpl* left-overs

sobrasada (sobrassada) *nf* sausage variety

sobre *prep* on, over

sobreabundancia *nf* glut

sobrecarga *nf* surcharge

sobrecontrata *nf* overbooking

sobremesa *nf* tablecloth; pudding; **de ~** after-lunch; after-dinner; **estar de ~** linger after lunch

sobreprecio *nm* surcharge

sobretasa *nf* surcharge

sobrio *a* frugal; sober

sobros *nmpl* left-overs

soconusco *nm* high-quality chocolate

soda *nf* soda water; [CAmer] coffee bar; **~ con helado** ice-cream soda

soflamar *vt* to singe

sofreír *vt* to lightly fry; to sauté; to sweat

sofrito *nm* onion/garlic/tomato sauce-base; *a* lightly fried

soja *nf* (of bean) soya; **semilla de ~** soya bean

sol *nm* sun; **~ y sombra** brandy/anisette cocktail

solera *nf* (of wine) vintage

soleta *nf* wafer; sponge-cake finger; ladyfinger

solido *a* solid

solla *nf* plaice

sollo *nm* sturgeon

solo *a* alone; on its own; (of tea/coffee) black; (of whisky &c) neat, straight, on its own

solo *nm* black coffee

solomillo *nm* sirloin steak; fillet steak; tenderloin

soltar *vt* (of cooking smells &c) to give off; (of meat juices &c) to ooze from

soluble *a* soluble; (of coffee) instant

solysombra *nm* (of drink) brandy/anisette

sombra *nf* shade; sunshade, parasol

sombrerero *nm* [SCone, Andes] hat-stand

sombrilla *nf* sunshade

sombrío *a* shady

somontano *nm* spanish wine variety

sopa *nf* soup; **~ juliana (~ de verduras)** vegetable soup; **~ (seco)** [Mex] second course; **~ chilena** [Andes] potato/maize soup; **~ de rabo de buey (~ de cola (buey))** oxtail soup;

sopaipilla *nf* [Andes, SCone] fritter

sopar (sopear) *vt* (of bread) to dunk

sope *nm* [Mex] spicy sauced

beans/onion tortilla

sopera *nf* soup tureen

sopero *a* soup; *nm* soup plate

sorber *vt* to soak up, to absorb

sorbete *nm* sorbet, sherbet; [Carib, SCone] (of drinks) straw

sorbetería *nf* ice-cream parlour

sorbetón *nm* mouthful

sorbito *nm* sip

sorbo *nm* sip

sorgo *nm* sorghum

sorpresa *nf* surprise

sorrasear *vt* to part roast

sosa *nf* soda; **~ cáustica** caustic soda

soso *a* unsalted; tasteless

sostenerse *vpr* (of food) to sustain oneself; to fortify oneself

soufflé *nm* soufflé

soya *nf* [LatAm] soya

spaghetti(s) (spaguetti(s)) *nmpl* spaghetti

store *nm* awning

strogonoff *a* (of beef) strogonoff; onion/mushroom-garnished cream-sauced

strudel *nm* strudel; thin filled pastry case

suave *a* (of taste) mild; (of temperature) moderate

submarino *nm* [Ar] hot milk/slab of chocolate

suchi *a* (of salad) bean shoot

sucrosa *nf* sucrose

suculencia *nf* succulence; tastiness,

suculento *a* succulent; tasty

sudado *nm* [Peru] stew

suela *nf* sea fish: sole

suelto *a* (of money) coins; loose change

suero *nm* (of milk) whey; **~ de leche** butter milk

suflé *nm* soufflé

suizo *nm* sugared bun

sumergir *vt* to immerse; to dunk

sumiller *nm* wine waiter; sommelier

superabundancia *nf* glut

supermercado *nm* supermarket

suplemental *a* supplementary

suplemento *nm* supplement

supremo *a* supreme

surtido *a* mixed; assorted

suruví (surubí) *nm* [SCone] freshwater fish: catfish

suspender *vt* to postpone; to cancel

suspiro *nm* [LatAm] meringue

sustancia *nf* essence; substance; **~ de carne** meat stock

suzettes (crepes) *a* (crêpes) suzettes; flambé-ed orange liquered

T

tabacalera *nf* cigar/cigarette case

tabacismo pasivo *nm* passive smoking

tabaco *nm* tobacco; cigarettes; [LatAm] cigar

tabaquera *nf* cigar/cigarette case

tabaquito *nm* [LatAm] small cigar

tabasco® *nm* Tabasco®

taberna *nf* inn; bar

tabernero (a) *nm/f* barman/ barmaid, bartender

tabla *nf* board; ~ **de amasar** bread/kneading board; ~ **de cocina** (~ **de picar**) chopping board; ~ **de quesos** cheeseboard

tableta *nf* (of chocolate) bar, slab

tablilla *nf* [Mex] (of chocolate) bar

taburete *nm* stool

taca (almeja) *nf* mollusc: clam variety

tacana *nf* [SCone] pestle

tacanear *vt* to crush

tacho *nm* pan

taco *nm* (of cheese &c) cube; [Mex] taco, rolled filled tortilla

tadorna *nf* sheldrake

tafia *nf* [LatAm] rum

tagarnina *nf* cheap cigar

taguara *nf* [Venez] cheap restaurant

tajada *nf* slice

tajar *vt* to slice, to chop, to cut

tallarín *nm* noodle

tallo *nm* [Andes] cabbage; ~**s** [LatAm] vegetables; greens; greenery; (of mushrooms &c) stalk; (of celery) stick; crystallized fruit

tamal *nm* [LatAm] tamale; highly spiced maize/meat

tamaño *nm* (of potato &c) size

támaras *nfpl* dates

tamarindo *nm* tamarind

tambo *nm* [Andes] wayside tavern

tamiz *nm* sieve

tamizado *a* sifted

tamizar *vt* to sift

tangerina *nf* tangerine

tanino *nm* tannin

tanta *nf* maize bread

tapa *nf* tapa; appetizers complimentary with beer; [Andes] rump steak; (of containers) lid; cap; top; ~ **de rosca** screw top; (of food) bar snack

tapadera *nf* lid; [Mex] (of bottle) top; cap

tapado *nm* meat stew; [Andes, CAmer] barbecued meat/ plantain dish

tapabarriga *nf* (of meat) flank

tapapecho *nm* (of beef) brisket; (of lamb) breast; (of pork) belly

tapar *vt* (of bottle) to cork; to cap; to cover; to lid; to fill

tapara *nf* [Carib] gourd, calabash

tapenade *nm* tapenade; olive/ anchovy/caper hors d'oeuvre

tapete *nm* tablecloth

tapetusa *nf* illicit spirits

tapioca *nf* tapioca

tapón *nm* top, cap; (of bottle) cork

taquear *vt* [Mex] to snack tacos

taquería *nf* [Mex] taco bar

taquilla *nf* [SCone] sweet surf clam

taquito *nm* (of meat &c) small cube

tarantín *nm* [CAmer, Carib] kitchen implement

tararira *nf* [Ar] freshwater fish: trahira

tarde *nf* afternoon; evening; **a las ocho de la ~** at eight o'clock in the evening

tarifa *nf* price list

tarjeta *nf* card; **~ de crédito** credit card; **~ de visita** business card; **~ dinero** cash-card; **~ telefónica** phonecard

tarragona *nm* spanish wine variety

tarro *nm* jar

tarta *nf* cake; tart; gâteau; **~ de bodas (~ nupcial)** wedding cake; **~ de cumpleaños** birthday cake; **~ de queso** cheesecake

tartaleta *nf* tartlet; slice of cake

tártaro *a* (of sauce) tartar

tartera *nf* cake tin; lunch box

tarugo *nm* (of stale bread) chunk

tasa *nf* rate; **~ de cambio** exchange rate

tasajo *nm* dried beef

tasca *nf* bar

tascar *vt* [Andes] to crunch

taxímetro *nf* [Arg] taxi

taza *nf* cup; cupful

tazón *nm* large cup; mug

té *nm* tea; tea party

tecito *nm* cup of tea

tecomate *nm* [CAmer] gourd, calabash; bowl

tehuacán *nm* [Mex] mineral water

tejeringo *nm* fritter

tejolote *nm* [Mex] pestle

tela *nf* [Andes] thin maize pancake; sieve

telebanco *nm* hole-in-the-wall; cash dispensing machine

telefacsímil (telefax) *nm* fax

teléfono *nm* telephone; **~ celular (móvil)** mobile

televisión *nf* television

telilla *nf* membrane; film; skin

témpano de tocino *nm* flitch of bacon

temperante *a* [LatAm] teetotal; *nm/f* [LatAm] teetotaller

temperatura *nf* temperature; **~ ambiente** room temperature

templado *a* luke-warm

templar *vt* (of mildness) to warm-up; to cool-down

temporada *nf* (of period) season

tempranero *a* (of fruit &c) early

tempranillo *nm* (of grape) spanish red

tenacillas *nfpl* (of sugar) tongs;

(of candles) snuffers

tenazas *nfpl* tongs

tenca *nf* tench

tender *vt* (of table) to lay

tendido *nm* batch of loaves

tendinoso *a* (of meat) stringy

tendón *nm* tendon

tenedor *nm* fork; (of restaurant rating) star

tentáculo *nm* tentacle

tentar *vt* to try

tenue *a* (of mesh) fine; (of smell) faint

tepalcate *nm* [CAmer, Mex] earthenware jug

tequila *nm* tequila; agave spirit

terciado *a* [LatAm] medium-sized; (of sugar) brown

terciar *vt* [LatAm] (of liquid) to dilute; [Mex] to blend, to mix

termidor *a* (of lobster) thermidor; mustard/bercy sauce-cooked au gratin/mornay sauce-served

terminar *vt* to finish

terminos *nmpl* (of meat &c) **¿qué ~?** How done (cooked) is it?

termo® *nm* vacuum flask

termómetro *nm* thermometer

ternera *nf* veal; (of cattle) calf

terra alta *nm* spanish wine variety

terracota *nf* terracotta

terraza *nf* terrace/pavement café; two handled jug

terrina *nf* terrine

terrón *nm* (of sugar) lump

tetera *nf* teapot; **~ eléctrica** electric kettle

tetilla *nf* cone-shaped Galician cheese

textura *nf* texture

tibio *a* tepid, lukewarm

tiburón *nm* shark variety; **~ bacota** bacota shark; **~ cazón** tope shark; **~ escalandrún** bull shark; **~ gatopardo** seven gilled shark; **~ gatuzo** patagonian smoothhound; **~ de río** freshwater fish: pike

tiempo *nm* time

tienda *nf* shop

tiento *nm* taste

tierno *a* (of meat) tender; (of bread &c) fresh; (of celery &c) young; tender

tiesto *nm* tin; container

tigre *nm* [Andes] black coffee with a drop of milk; [Andes] cocktail

tila *nf* lime blossom tea

tilo *nm* [LatAm] lime blossom tea

timbal *nm* meat pie

timbusca *nf* [Andes] spicy soup; spiced regional dish

tina *nf* (of wine) vat

tino *nm* vat

tinta *nf* (of squid &c) ink

tintillo *nm* [SCone] red wine

tinto *a* (of wine) red; *nm* red wine; (of glass) red wine; (of cup) black coffee

tintorera *nf* shark

tintorro *nm* red plonk

tipo *nm* type; kind; sort

tira nf rib; strip

tirabuzón nm corkscrew

tiramizú nm tiramizu; coffee/sponge/cream-cheese pick-me-up

tirar vt to discard; to throw away

tirita nf (of presentation) decoration; appendage

tisana nf tisane, herbal tea

titre nm sea fish: Pacific menhaden

tlachique nm [Mex] unfermented pulque

tlascal nm [Mex] tortilla

tocado a (of food) off; bad; toilet, WC

toche nm [Mex] hare

tocineta nf [Colom] bacon

tocinillo de cielo nm egg yolk/syrup pudding

tocino nm lard; bacon; salt pork; ~ **entreverado (~ veteado)** streaky bacon; ~ **de cielo** egg yolk/syrup pudding

todo a all

tofu (tofú) nm tofu, soya bean curd

toilette nm [SCone] WC, toilet

tol nm gourd

toldo nm marquee; (of beach) sunshade

tollo nm sea fish: shark variety

tomar vt to take; (of food/drink) to have; to eat/drink

tomate nm tomato

tomillo nm thyme; ~ **salsero** savory

tomoyo nm sea fish: tomoyo cinid

tonel nm barrel

tonelete nm keg

tongo nm rum punch

tongorí nm [Andes, SCone] liver; lights; offal

tónica nf tonic water

topocho nm [Carib] plantain

torcedura nf weak wine

torcer vt (of milk &c) to go off

tordo nm (of bird) thrush

toremo nm sea fish: amberjack

torete nm young bull

tornasol nm sunflower

toro nm bull; spanish wine variety

toronja nf grapefruit, pomelo

torrados nmpl toasted chickpeas

torrar vt to toast; roast

torrefacción nf toasting; roasting

torreja nf [LatAm] fried fruit/vegetable slices; [SCone] slice of fruit

torrezno nm (of bacon) rasher

torrificar vt [Mex] (of coffee) to roast

torrija nf sweet milk-ed bread wined and battered; slice of French toast

torta nf pancake; tart; cake; flan, sponge cake; [Mex] sandwich; ~ **de hojarasca** layered cake; ~ **de huevos** omelette; ~ **de crema** custard pie

tortilla *nf* (of eggs) omelette; ~
español potato omelette, ~
francesa plain omelette;
[CAmer, Mex] maize pancake;
tortilla

tortita *nf* pancake

toscano *nm* cigar variety

tostada *nf* slice of toast; ~**s**
toast, [Mex] fried maize tortilla;
[CAmer] toasted banana; ~
delgada Melba toast

tostado *a* toasted; (of coffee)
roasted; *nm* toasted sandwich

tostador *nm* (of bread) toaster;
(of coffee) roaster

tostadora *nf* toaster

tostar *vt* (of bread) to toast; (of
meat) to brown; (of coffee) to
roast

tostón *nm* crouton; (of toast)
oil-dunked toast; roast sucking
pig; [Carib] fried green banana

totopo *nm* [CAmer, Mex] tortilla
chip

totoposte *nm* [CAmer, Mex]
tortilla chip

totuma *nf* [Andes, Carib] gourd,
calabash

trabajar *vt* (of ingredient) to
work

trabajo *nm* (of meal) working
meal

trabar *vt* (of sauce/liquid) to
thicken

tradición *nf* tradition

tragadero *nm* gullet

tragar *vt* to swallow

trago *nm* alcoholic or non-
alcoholic drink

tranquilo *a* (of wine) non-
sparkling; still; (of ambience)
peaceful

transformación *nf* processing

transgénico *a* genetically
modified

trapicar *vi* [SCone] to taste hot

trapo *nm* cleaning cloth

traposo *a* [SCone] stringy;
tough

traquear *vt* [Carib] to drink

trascocina *nf* scullery

trascolar *vt* to strain

trasegar *vt* to decant

trasvasar *vt* to decant

trébedes *nfpl* trivet

trebejos de cocina *nmpl* (of
kitchen) utensils

trenza *nf* plait; twist

tres *a* three; third

trigo *nm* wheat; ~ **entero**
wholemeal

triguero *nm* wheat

trinchar *vt* (of meat) to chop up;
to carve

trinche *nm* [LatAm] fork

trinchete *nm* [Andes] table
knife

tripas *nfpl* intestine; (of fruit)
seeds, core

tripicallos *nmpl* tripe

tritre (machuelo) *nm* sea fish:
Pacific menhaden

triturador *nm* mincer; ~ **de ajo**
garlic crusher

triturar *vt* to crush; to grind

trocear *vt* to cut into pieces

trocito *nm* piece

trola *nf* [Andes] slice of ham

trona *nf* high-chair

troncha *nf* [LatAm] slice; [Mex] sparse meal

tronco de Navidad *nm* yule log

tropezones *nmpl* (of soup) chunky additions; embellishments

tropical *a* tropical

trozar *vt* to cut up

trozo *nm* piece

trucha *nf* trout; ~ **arco iris** freshwater fish: rainbow trout; ~ **maina** migratory fish: sea trout; ~ **marrón** brown trout

truchero *a* trout

trufa *nf* truffle

trufado *a* truffled

trufar *vt* to truffle

trullo *nm* teal

trutro *nm* (of chicken) thigh

tualé *nm/f* toilet, WC

tubérculo *nm* potato; tuber

tubo *nm* tube

tuco *nm* [SCone] (of pasta) sauce; tomato sauce

tueste *nm* roasting; toasting

tuétano *nm* marrow

tumba *nf* [SCone] cheap stew

tumbao *nm* [SCone] (of mollusc) Chilean semele

tumbo *nm* passion fruit

tuna *nf* prickly pear; [Chile] melon

túnido *nm* sea fish: tuna

tupinambo *nm* Jerusalem artichoke

turba *nf* peat

turbante *nm* [Mex] gourd, calabash

turbar *vt* to stir

turbot *nm* sea fish: turbot

turma *nf* truffle; [Andes] potato

turrón *nm* nougat

tusa (tuse [SCone] *nm) nf* [CAmer, Andes] (of maize) cob

tutti frutti *nm* tutti frutti; all-fruit; mixed fruit in various forms

tutuma *nf* cucumber variety

U

ubre *nf* udder

ulerear *vt* [SCone] to roll out

ulero *nm* [SCone] rolling pin

ulluco *nm* manioc

ulpo *nm* maize soup; [Chile] sugar/roasted flour cold drink

ulte *nm* seaweed variety

último (a) *a nm/f* last

ultracongelado *a* [Spain] deep-frozen

ultracongelador *nm* [Spain] freezer

ultracongelar *vt* [Spain] to deep-freeze

ultramarinos *nmpl* groceries; grocer's

unidad *nf* units; **dos ~es** for two

unir *vt* to blend; to mix

uno *a* one

untar *vt* to spread; to soak; to dunk; to dip; (of cake tin) to grease

unto nm lard

uperizado a (of milk) UHT

urogallo nm capercaillie; large grouse

urta nf sea bream

uslerear vt (of pastry) to roll out

uslero nm [Chile] rolling pin

utensilio nm utensil

uva nf grape; wine; drink; ~ **blanca** green/white grape; ~ **crespa (~ espina)** gooseberry; ~ **de Corinto** currant; ~ **pasa** raisin; ~ **moscatel** muscatel grape; ~ **pasa** raisin, ~**s de mesa** dessert grapes

V

vaca nf cow; (of meat) beef

vacación nf holiday(s)

vaccinio nm [Spain] blueberry, bilberry

vaciar vt (of bottle &c) to empty

vacío a empty; [CAmer, Carib, Andes] (of bread) dry

vacuno a bovine

vagón restaurante nm dining car

vaho nm steam

vaina nf pod; ~**s** green beans; port/sherry cocktail

vainilla nf vanilla

vainita nf [LatAm] green beans

vajilla nf crockery; dinner service; dishes

valdiviano nm vegetable/dried meat dish

valdeorras nm spanish wine variety

valdepeñas nm spanish wine variety

vale de comida nm lunch voucher

valencia nm spanish wine variety

valenciana nf small cake; **a la ~** riced seafood; [Chile] chicken/ frankfurter/seafood/pork-rib/ peppers/onion-garnished

valer vt to cost

valor nm (calorific/nutritional) value

valva nf (of mollusc) valve

vapor nm steam

vaporearse vpr to evaporate

vaquería nf dairy

varajillo nm [Carib] liqueur coffee

variantes nmpl pickled crudités

vasca (a la) a (of rice) bacon/ sausage/tomato/peppers/ onion/olive-garnished

vasija nf dish

vaso nm glass; tumbler; [Andes] small cup; glassful

vástago nm shoot; sprout

veda nf (of game) close season

vegetal a vegetable; ~**es** nmpl [CAmer] vegetables; **carbón ~** charcoal

vegetariano (a) nm/f, a vegetarian

veguero nm cigar

vejiga *nf* bladder

vela *nf* candle

velada *nf* party; soirée

veladora *nf* [LatAm] candle

venado *nm* venison

vendimia *nf* (of wine) vintage

venera *nf* scallop; scallop shell

venero *nm* (of water) spring

venirse *vpr* (of bread-mix) to prove; (of wine) to ferment

ventorrillo *nm* small inn

verano *nm* summer; dry season

verde *a* green; (of bean) green; (of fruit) green, unripe; *nm* [SCone] maté; [SCone] salad; [Andes] plantain

verdear *vi* [SCone] to drink maté

verdulería *nf* greengrocer's

verdura *nf* greens; vegetables

verificar *vt* (of salt &c) to test; to check; to taste

vermú (vermut) *nm* vermouth

veronica *a* (of pudding) whisky/lemon/condensed-milk dessert

verraco *nm* boar; [Andes] ram

verter *vt* (of liquids) to pour; to empty out into

veteado *a* (of bacon &c) streaky

vianda *nf* food; [Carib] vegetables; [SCone] packed lunch

viciar *vt* (of meal) to spoil

vid *nf* vine

vidriado *nm* glazed pottery

vidriera *nf* [Carib] tobacco kiosk

vidrio *nm* glass; [SCone] bottle of spirits; (of drink) glass

vidriola *nf* sea fish: fortune jack

vieira *nf* mollusc: scallop

vieja (mulata) *nf* sea fish: wrasse

viejo *a* old

vienesa *nf* [Chile] frankfurter

vientre *nm* stomach

viernes *nm/adv* Friday

vigorizante *a* (of drink) stimulating

vijúa *nf* [Andes] rock salt

vinagre *nm* vinegar

vinagrera *nf* vinegar bottle; ~s cruet

vinagreta (salsa) *nf* vinaigrette, French dressing

vinagroso *a* acid-tasting

vinazo *nm* strong wine

vínico *a* wine

vino *nm* wine; ~ de aguja (~ espumoso) sparkling wine; ~ del año new wine; ~ blanco white wine; ~ de casa house wine; ~ corriente (~ peleón) plonk; ~ de jerez sherry; ~s de madrid spanish wine variety; ~ de mesa table wine; ~ de Oporto port; drinks; reception; ~ de postre pudding wine; ~ de reserva reserve; ~ rosado rosé wine; ~ de solera vintage wine; ~ tinto red wine; ~ tranquilo still wine

viña *nf* vineyard

viñal *nm* [SCone] vineyard
viñedo *nm* vineyard
virote *nm* [Mex] bread-roll
vísceras *nfpl* guts
vitamina *nf* vitamin
vitaminada (vitaminizado) *a* with added vitamins
vitícola *a* grape; (of region) wine-producing
viticultura *nf* viticulture
viuda *nf* [Andes] fish stew
vodka *nm* vodka
volador *nm* sea fish: flying fish; squid
volcar *vt* to turn out (onto)
volován *nm* vol-au-vent
volumen *nm* (of liquids) volume
volver *vt* to turn over; (of milk) to turn, to go off
vuelo *nm* wings
vuelta y vuelta *nf* (of steak &c) rare

W

wafle *nm* [LatAm] waffle
wáter *nm* toilet, lavatory, WC
whiskería (wisquería) *nf* bar
whisky ([Irish] whiskey) *nm* whisky, whiskey; **whisky de malta** malt whisky

X

xanfaina (chanfaina) *nf* onion/peppers/vegetables sauce

Y

yac (yak) *nm* yak
yantar *vt* to eat, to lunch; *nm* food
yecla *nm* spanish wine variety
yema *nf* egg yolk, [LatAm] egg; egg yolk/sugar sweet; ~ **mejida** eggnog; ~ **de Santa Teresa** soft creamed confection
yerba (de) mate *nf* maté; herbal tea-like drink
yerbabuena *nf* [LatAm] mint
yerbear *vi* [SCone] to drink maté
yeros *nmpl* lentils
yesca *nf* thirst-inducing food
yesquero *nm* [LatAm] cigarette lighter
yogur *nm* yoghurt; ~ **descremado (~ desnatado)** low-fat yoghurt
yuca *nf* [LatAm] manioc root, cassava; [Andes] food
yuyo *nm* [Peru, RPlate] herbal tea

Z

zacate *nm* [Mex] teacloth
zanahoria *nf* carrot
zapallito *nm* [SCone] courgette
zapallo *nm* gourd, pumpkin; [Chile] marrow; courgette
zapatero *a* (of vegetables) hard; undercooked
zapote *nm* (of fruit) sapodilla

plum; naseberry

zaranda *nf* sieve

zarazo *a* [LatAm] (of fruit)
underripe

zaro *nm* (of maize) cob

zarzamora *nf* blackberry

zarzaparrilla *nf* sarsaparilla

zarzuela de mariscos *nf*
seafood stew

zocato *a* (of fruit &c) hard; *nm*
stale bread

zona *nf* area; ~ **de picnic** picnic
area; ~ **franca** duty-free zone

zorzal *nm* (of bird) thrush

zumbo *nm* [CAmer, Andes]
gourd, calabash

zumiento *a* juicy

zumo *nm* fruit juice

zumoso *a* juicy

zupia *nf* [Andes] badly-made
spirits

zurito *nm* (of beer) small
glassful

zurrapa *nf* (of coffee) grounds